A Student's Guide to AS Drama and Theatre Studies

for the **AQA** Specification

by

Robert Lowe and Philip Rush

Rhinegold Publishing Ltd
241 Shaftesbury Avenue
London WC2H 8TF
Telephone: 01832 270333
Fax: 01832 275560
www.rhinegold.co.uk

Rhinegold Drama and Theatre Studies Study Guides
A Student's Guide to AS Drama and Theatre Studies for the AQA Specification
A Student's Guide to A2 Drama and Theatre Studies for the AQA Specification

A Student's Guide to AS Drama and Theatre Studies for the Edexcel Specification
A Student's Guide to A2 Drama and Theatre Studies for the Edexcel Specification

Rhinegold Performance Studies Study Guides
A Student's Guide to AS Performance Studies for the OCR Specification
A Student's Guide to A2 Performance Studies for the OCR Specification

Other Rhinegold Study Guides
Student's Guides to GCSE, AS and A2 Music for the AQA, Edexcel and OCR Specifications
Listening Tests for Students for the AQA, Edexcel and OCR GCSE Music Specifications
A Student's Guide to Music Technology for the Edexcel AS and A2 Specification
Student's Guides to AS and A2 Religious Studies for the AQA, Edexcel and OCR Specifications

Rhinegold Publishing also publishes Classical Music, Early Music Today, Music Teacher, Opera Now, Piano, The Singer, British and International Music Yearbook, British Performing Arts Yearbook, Music Education Yearbook, Rhinegold Dictionary of Music in Sound.

First published 2004 in Great Britain by
Rhinegold Publishing Ltd
241 Shaftesbury Avenue
London WC2H 8TF
Telephone: 01832 270333
Fax: 01832 275560
www.rhinegold.co.uk
© Rhinegold Publishing Ltd
Reprinted 2004

You should always check the current requirements of the examination, since these may change. Copies of the AQA Specification may be obtained from the Publications Department, AQA, Aldon House, 39 Heald Grove, Rusholme, Manchester M14 4NA
See also the AQA website at www.aqa.org.uk

A Student's Guide to AS Drama and Theatre Studies for the AQA Specification
British Library Cataloguing in Publication Data.
A catalogue record for this book is available from the British Library.
ISBN 1-904226-27-2
Printed in Great Britain by The Friary Press

Contents

The authors

Robert Lowe has been the director of the Stahl Theatre and head of drama at Oundle School for the past 10 years. He serves as the reviser for AQA AS and A2 theatre studies and is a team leader and examiner of many years standing of both written and practical components at all levels. Prior to his teaching career Robert was a professional actor for a number of years, and still combines professional appearances with his teaching career.

Philip Rush is an assistant headteacher at St Peter's High School, Gloucester, where he teaches in the English department. He has taught theatre studies for 20 years and also led the postgraduate training scheme for trainee English and drama teachers at the University of Gloucestershire in Cheltenham for seven years. He has a degree in English from Westfield College, University of London and an MA in drama from Bristol University where he is currently studying for a diploma in creative writing. He has performed at the Edinburgh Festival fringe and has toured with one of his own plays, which focused on the Irish famine. His poems have been published in a number of magazines including *Poetry Review*.

Acknowledgements

In the writing of a guide such as this many people have contributed. The authors and publishers are grateful to the following people for their specific advice, support and expert contributions: Hallam Bannister, Nina Crowe, Joanna Hughes, Lucien Jenkins, John Nicol, Charlotte Regan, Nic Saunders, Abigail Walmsley, Sarah Williams and Emma Whale. The authors are also conscious of having drawn on a lifetime's reading. More recently the growth in use of the Internet has made an unparalleled amount of exciting information and challenging opinion widely available. Although every attempt has been made to acknowledge both the primary and secondary sources drawn on, it is impossible to do justice to the full range of material that has shaped the creation of this book. The authors would therefore like to apologise if anyone's work has not been properly acknowledged. They would be happy to hear from authors or publishers so that any such errors or omissions may be rectified in future editions.

Introduction

Theatre is a passion for those of us who work in drama, whether on stage or behind the scenes, whether as a director or a designer, or indeed as a teacher. It is a passion that has caught hold of us at some stage and will not let go. We would hope that you have chosen to study drama and theatre studies at AS level because you too are discovering that you have a passion for theatre. Certainly one of the most vital ingredients for successful completion of this course is an enthusiasm for going to the theatre and for taking part. It doesn't matter whether your interests within theatre are narrow or broad at this stage, though we hope that as you continue to study drama you will find new aspects of it that you had not appreciated before, as long as you are interested in finding out how theatre works.

Why drama?

This guide is intended to provide assistance to students of AQA AS drama and theatre studies. It will take you through the various elements of the course and explain the precise requirements of each unit, offering guidance as to what the examiners are looking for. However, no book on drama can take the place of practical experience. This is a subject that requires a hands-on approach; indeed a large percentage of the final result is based on practical work. In addition, much of your work will rely on other members of your class, and they will rely on you. This will require such skills as communication and team-building. Throughout the book we will be offering ideas for practical work that should be shared with your colleagues and experienced in class together. Drama and theatre studies is possibly the only subject you will be taking whereby your result is dependent on the work of others and in which your work can affect others' grades. It is thus vital that you are able to work well with your colleagues and have the same aims. All theatre is the result of teamwork and it is only right that this is reflected in the examination.

Teamwork

Much of the course is concerned with discovering how to transfer words from the page into words on stage: what happens to the drama text as a group of people get hold of it and begin to fashion a piece of live theatre from it. It also includes the task of writing or devising a piece of theatre from scratch. This guide will give you plenty of ideas on how to approach each task of the exam. It follows a format of constantly asking you questions, with the intention of leading you to find solutions to the problems that arise as you start to think about producing theatre. It is this idea of solving problems that you should find most useful as you work towards the exam, whether it be along the lines of 'how do I create a set that will encompass both a royal palace and a mysterious wood?' or 'how do I show the audience that I am feeling angry at this moment in the text?' or 'how did the director manage to create that feeling of tension at that point in the production?'

Solving problems

See pages 13–26.

We have included a reference chapter concerning those theatrical terms and ideas that you will need to be able to refer to with confidence in your essays. 'Understanding Theatre' also includes a list of the common staging forms with diagrams, which should be helpful when working on the units Approaches to Text and Theatre in Practice.

The AS modules

Unit 1: Devised Drama – Practical (40%)

You are required to work in groups of between four and eight to create and present an original piece of drama for an audience. The piece of theatre should last between 15 and 30 minutes depending on the size of the group.

Inspiration for the piece should be drawn from the content of the AS course. This inspiration may influence the content or the style of the presentation. There must be clear dramatic intentions for the audience. Each group is totally responsible for every aspect of the piece of drama created.

You must nominate individually a specific skill that you will demonstrate during the final presentation. These skills are: acting, costume design and construction, mask design and construction, design and execution of stage setting(s), and the technical elements of lighting and/or sound. If all the members of your group are nominating acting as their specialist skill, the whole group must share responsibility for all the production elements relating to the final piece.

As part of the process you must present a portfolio, which details the process of the creation of the devised piece, outlining in particular your own contribution to the genesis and development of the piece. If you have nominated a design skill your portfolio should include sketches and diagrams. In addition your teacher will assess your general preparation, development and analysis of the work in progress. This accounts for 10 per cent, the portfolio for a further 10 per cent, and the final performance for 20 per cent of your final, total AS mark. Your teacher will mark the final performance, but an external moderator will be present on the day of the performance to assess some of the groups in your centre and to check that your teacher is marking at the agreed level.

Unit 2: Approaches to Text – Written (30%)

Here you will be assessed on your study of two plays in a one-and-a-half hour written examination, which will be marked externally. There are two sections in this unit:

➤ Section A: The Greeks to the Jacobeans

➤ Section B: The Twentieth Century and Contemporary Drama

You will study one play for each of these sections and you will be required to answer one question for each play. The performance perspective is central to this unit, and you must focus on the interpretation of each play from the point of view of either the actor, the designer or the director. You must also take into account the original social and theatrical contexts of the plays.

Currently (until 2006) the choice of texts is as follows:

Set texts

Section A: The Greeks to the Jacobeans:
• Sophocles – *Antigone*
• Shakespeare – *A Midsummer Night's Dream*
• Jonson – *Volpone*
• Middleton – *The Changeling*

Section B: The 20th Century and Contemporary Drama
• Chekhov – *Three Sisters*
• O'Casey – *The Shadow of a Gunman*
• Lorca – *Yerma*
• Bond – *Restoration*

You will be allowed access to annotated texts in the exam room.

For more on this, see page 51.

Unit 3: Theatre in Practice – Written (30%)

This module comes in two parts.

➤ Section A (Section B in 2004): Response to live productions

In 2004, as has previously been the case, the two sections will be assessed on the same paper, with questions on your chosen practitioners first, followed by questions on your response to live theatre. From 2005 onwards, these sections will be assessed in two separate exams. This is why they are represented by two distinct chapters (Theatre in Practice – Practitioners, and Theatre in Practice – Response to Live Theatre) in this guide.

You are required to give a personal response to various aspects of live theatre observed during your course. You must answer one question from a choice of four on one production that you have seen, excluding any play that is prescribed as a set text at either AS or A2 by the exam board. You will be expected to refer to aspects of directorial interpretation and to the range of production elements employed within the production. You will be allowed to take brief personal notes on productions you have seen into the exam room to help you. You are allowed two sides of A4 notes on each production, and you will have 45 minutes to answer your chosen question.

➤ Section B (Section A in 2004): Practitioners

You are required to study the theory and practices of **one** of the following three theatre practitioners:

◆ Stanislavski

◆ Artaud

◆ Craig

You will be required to answer one question from a choice of four, demonstrating your knowledge and understanding of the work and the significance of your selected practitioner. One question will be set on each practitioner; the fourth question may be answered with reference to any one of the three practitioners.

How to approach the course

Writing essays

You should always write a very personal response to whatever question you are answering. It is *your* understanding and assessment of how theatre works in practice that matters. One of the dangers for those candidates who are also studying the more formal essay-based subjects such as English or history is that they feel they must write equally dispassionate essays for drama and theatre studies. This is not the case. One way to get yourself out of this habit is to begin every essay you write during the initial stages of your course with the word 'I'. This way your opinion will immediately become important to your essay and indeed the focus of it.

Another method is to speak your essays aloud. They should sound as if you are talking to someone about your theatre experiences rather than as if you are reading from a book. Theatre is a very personal and, as we've already noted, a very passionate thing. You must convey this passion and enthusiasm through your written work. Examiners want to recognise that you have enjoyed as well as learnt from your course. This attitude should be evident in all the written work you do, from your portfolio to your response to live productions.

Taking notes

It is very important that throughout your course you keep comprehensive notes of all that you do, whether it be your own personal research from background reading, or from practical class work. It is all too easy to get caught up with practical exercises and explorations of text and not give yourself time to write up that work in note form. You should always allow time for this, whether at the end of a class or in your own time soon after. If you don't do this you will forget the result of that practical work. This is obviously important when working on Unit 1, but is equally so for the other units too.

Your teacher will hopefully allow for this in class, but if not then you must find the time to keep your notes up to date in your own time. Keep loose-leaved files on all the sections of the exam. You will find that the work you do for one unit will directly relate to work done for a different unit. Thus when studying how to approach a text as a director you will find that this directly relates to your study of live productions. It is likely that the work you do on your chosen practitioner will also relate to the work you do when preparing your piece of devised theatre for Unit 1.

Writing in the exam

In each chapter of this guide (with the exception of the reference section), you will find sample exam questions so that you may test yourself. You will also find some ideas on how to answer a question in the exam. But it may also be useful for you to see what a high-grade response to such a question might look like, so that you can get an idea of strong essay technique. The following is a genuine student response to a question from the response to live productions module. It is a strong answer with a clear structure, which focuses clearly on the question asked. The amount of detail is impressive in places, and you should find that as you read the essay you can picture these performances, even though it is extremely unlikely that you saw the production.

There are comments about the answer in the margin, which should help you to see where the quality lies.

Sample question

With reference to ONE production that you have seen, discuss how two of the performers used their skills in order to portray character.

Student response

The Laramie Project, by Moises Kaufman and the Tectonic Theatre Company, was a docu-drama performed at the Stahl Theatre in February 2003 by a local student company. The script was composed from a series of interviews with real people, all of whom were connected in some way to Matthew Shepard, the gay victim of a vicious hate crime in Laramie, Wyoming in 1998. This was a Brechtian, socio-political piece of theatre, in Epic style, split into many short scenes that were not necessarily in strict chronological order, and which together produced a play that asked its audience to reflect on the nature of tolerance and forgiveness within society, perhaps hoping that members of the audience would change their own views on such matters and indeed even go out and persuade others to change their views.

> Clear, concise summation of the production, stating the title, playwright, date, venue and company. Gives the context and style of the piece.

> Gives the interpretation and aims of the production.

The 10 actors took on over 60 roles throughout the performance, playing both the interviewers and the interviewees. The actors all remained on stage throughout the performance as themselves, observing the action and only becoming the different characters as they stood up and joined the action. Thus we had to accept them as many different characters while being made aware at all times that they were actors taking on roles. The audience watched them change roles by using their acting skills of voice and movement without the advantage of a change of costume other than an occasional item such as a hat or scarf. The intention of this was that we would not become too emotionally involved in the characters and situations in order that we could concentrate on and judge the issues of the play. I found this extremely effective, although the subject matter of the play did elicit an emotional response from me at times, as I found I often had an immediate strong reaction to the characters, which showed how successful the actors were in using their skills to create them.

> Sets out the concept of multi-role acting and the need for the actors to focus on their skills in portraying character.

One of the actors, James Inman, played seven roles, and the differences between them were particularly impressive. It was always immediately clear which of his many roles he was portraying

> Moves to first performer – stating name of the actor (often missed by candidates). Focuses on his skills and gives a personal evaluation.

Describes clearly the way the actor established this character referring to both physical and vocal work, using the correct terminology.

A particular and precise example given.

Offers a personal reflection on the character and the actor's skill.

Contrasting performance offered to show multi-role work – again precise detail offered.

Uses a complex piece of theatrical terminology correctly here. Gestus is a Brechtian term referring to a gesture or pose that sums up the attitude of an actor towards the character they are play-

Refers to what the actor did on stage and how that reveals character.

Again a precise moment of the performance discussed in detail.

due to his excellent acting skills, both physical and vocal. His first character, Jedediah Schultz, was a drama student at the University of Wyoming who talks of his and his parents' perceptions of gay people. Each time he appeared in this role he brought a chair to the front of the stage and turned it around, sitting on it the wrong way around, leaning on the back and facing the audience. To show the character physically he leant forwards and gesticulated a lot with his arms and hands, conveying the character's enthusiasm and energy for his opinions to the audience. Vocally Inman used a high pitch with an excited tone whenever he spoke, even when the character was criticising his parents, in order to bring out the strong views he held on the matter. Inman used a clear Wyoming accent to show the character's background and used emphasis well to convey his particular passions. For example, he called Laramie a 'beautiful town' and said the word 'beautiful' both higher and slower to show he really meant this. Inman's facial expression showed a wide-eyed look of innocence, which together with his leaning forward on the chair and direct address to us, meant he had a strong connection with the audience. I felt great sympathy for this character and his difficult relationship with his parents, which was undoubtedly due to Inman's excellent use of his acting skills.

In direct contrast with this character was the way Inman played one of the accused, Aaron McKinney. Inman's gestus for this was to rise from his seat, place his hands firmly in his pockets and stand very thin, but slouched forward with a scowl on his face. We immediately knew this was an unconfident, but unpleasant, character from this stance. The actor was providing us with a snapshot of the character and his own attitude towards him through this posture. Throughout the play Inman wore jeans and a grey tee-shirt and so in order to distinguish this character the only costume change was a beanie hat pulled down nearly over the eyes, but this was enough to make the change of character absolutely clear as it gave him a dark and dangerous look. This character appeared only once in the play, in an interview with the detective

during which he made his confession. Throughout the scene, Inman kept his eyes focused on the floor, making no eye contact with either the detective or the audience, showing an anti-social character and one we should not trust. His right leg had a constant shake and he fidgeted with his hands to show the character's nerves, but Inman also slumped back in his chair at times to show that McKinney was trying to act 'cool' during the interview, as though he didn't care about his crime, which I found a particularly effective portrayal of complicated feelings.

Inman's voice was low pitched and aggressive in tone, and he spoke generally in a monotonic American accent throughout the scene. At one point, when the character was told he was going to court that day, Inman sat up straight and raised his eyes, making eye-contact with the detective for the only time in the scene, showing McKinney's surprise and also fear at being given this information. I found the balance between the aggressive nature and the defensive posture very effective in conveying this troubled character, so that one almost had sympathy for him despite the awful nature of his crime.

For each of his roles Inman created a completely different posture and tone of voice, all of which were highly effective and clear throughout. It was hard at times to accept this was the same actor as he managed to transform himself completely and so successfully each time. In brief, among others he also played the streetwise, New York Italian actor, who constantly had a cigarette hanging from his lips and walked with a sexy swagger; the young boy who found the body, clearly deeply upset by the experience, shown through a slight stammer and awkward, gangly body movements; and a middle aged gay man reflecting on what had happened to the town since the crime, who possessed a calm, warm tone of voice and smooth, fluid gestures. I thought Inman was a consummate actor with highly developed skills.

Tom McLeod also played a variety of roles equally effectively. He first played Greg Pierotti, a member of the acting company interviewing the residents of Laramie, who was a thirty-something gay man. McLeod played him with a gentle, approachable manner. He stood with his jacket slung over his shoulder held by one finger, one leg slightly bent and relaxed, giving the impression of an easygoing character. He spoke softly with a low pitch and slight New York accent to suggest both the character's background and his sexuality. McLeod would look at the audience occasionally with very open eyes, raising his eyebrows, in order to show Pierotti's reaction to some of the answers he got during his interviews. By doing this he established a very strong relationship with the audience, even on one occasion stepping down off the stage into the auditorium and looking directly at us when the character he was interviewing used an expression Pierotti didn't understand, showing us his confusion and this allowed us to feel at one with him about the strange woman he was talking to. I found it very easy to warm to this character because of McLeod's clear portrayal of him.

In contrast to this character he also played Fred Phelps, an anti-gay protestor. This was a very angry character and one with whom the audience should have no sympathy; we should understand clearly that his views are bigoted and unacceptable in society. To create this, McLeod shouted directly at the audience using a strong, loud, Texan accent, while at the same time pointing at us and thus making us very uncomfortable. He waved his arms widely, using downward strokes, but standing with a wide stance showing a strength of purpose and self-importance, which was quite frightening in places. There was a violence about the character shown through this aggressive behaviour, added to which was McLeod's position right at the front of the stage, intimidating the audience, imposing and threatening. McLeod made this character seem so much taller than his other characters merely through his upright stance and presence, which was highly effective. He put huge emphasis on certain words such as 'you' when addressing us,

by speaking slower and raising his pitch and volume. McLeod was also able to hold direct eye contact with members of the audience in a completely different way from when he was acting Pierotti; the eyes seemed colder and much more threatening. This was a highly impressive display of an actor's skill.

Moves to the second performer – there is no requirement in this question to compare or contrast the two performers, though the candidate does this briefly later in the essay.

Discusses the actor's relationship with the audience, showing a strong awareness of the importance of this relationship in establishing and creating character.

Notice the way the candidate keeps referring to the key word (*skill*) in the question.

Like Inman, McLeod also played a number of other roles very effectively, each one being given a totally different body posture, set of gestures and voice. I particularly enjoyed his portrayal of the town detective, who seemed quite fat through the way McLeod walked with rather splayed feet and wider posture, and who constantly scratched his belly in a nonchalant but comic manner. Here was a character we liked immediately and found humorous; a great contrast to the vile Fred Phelps.

Overall I felt both these actors made the distinctions between their various characters extremely clearly. Although some of the characters only appeared for a short time in the play, they had obviously been thoroughly thought about, as they had great depth. It would have been easy to offer caricatures in this play, but these were real people given life upon the stage, which is a testament to the quality of these performers' skills. A hugely impressive achievement, and one from which I learnt a great deal about the nature of acting.

Here the candidate sums up. Note how they end their final paragraph.

Understanding Theatre

What is this chapter for?

Each A-level subject has its own basic terminology and concepts that are unique to it. To succeed in that subject, you need to be able to understand and employ these accurately and effectively. To understand the world of the theatre properly, there are some key ideas and terms that you must be aware of – you may have already come across some of them if you studied GCSE drama, or if you regularly take part in local productions. You will not be examined on the information in this chapter directly, but your comprehension of it is integral to your success.

Some of these terms and concepts are explained much more fully in later chapters, others are dealt with sufficiently here, and some could lead on to more thorough research. By using an internet search engine, you should be able to build on your enquiries.

Studying drama involves three distinct but closely related fields. Firstly, you will need to know about theatres, the places dedicated to the performing of plays. You need to know: how they are designed and how they work; how to describe their various features; and how lighting and scenic devices contribute to a production. In doing so, you will begin to learn about the history of drama and about the different kinds of plays which make up the European theatrical tradition. Secondly, you need to know about acting – in particular the theories that have emerged around the practice of preparing and presenting plays in performance. Finally, you need to be able to discuss play-texts subtly and professionally. For all this you will need a specialised vocabulary.

By familiarising yourselves with the specialist terms relating to the theatre, to acting and to the study of play-texts, you are familiarising yourselves with the foundations on which your study must be built. Reading this introduction will serve not only as a starting point to your work but also as a useful reminder as you progress, and finally as a revision aid when you face the examinations at the end of your studies.

Practical theatre and performance terms

Staging

European theatre began with the ancient Greeks and we still use a lot of their terms. The history of early drama is very closely linked to ancient Greek religion and religious festivities. It is sometimes useful to think of early theatres as a kind of open-air temple, where the audience was like a congregation and the performance a religious ritual. The name for the place where such performances took place was *theatron*. The *skene* was the wall behind the actors, which helped them project their voices; the *orchestra* was where

Greek theatre

Some people call these early theatres 'amphitheatres'. This is inaccurate. An amphitheatre was created from building two theatres facing each other to form something like a stadium.

the 'chorus' of dancers performed. There was probably a raised stage in front of the skene on which the actors stood, though they could move between this and the orchestra. It is thought that Sophocles introduced the idea of painting the skene to give some impression of setting. We use a Latin word for the area where the audience sits: *auditorium*.

Pageants

In medieval England, religious plays were performed on the feast of Corpus Christi which falls in early summer when the days are at their longest. During the day, in cities such as York and Wakefield, the guilds would perform a series of plays that enacted the entire story of the Bible. The audience took up its place along a route around the town, and the plays moved around during the day, so that by staying at one point, anyone could see the entire series, or cycle, of plays. These plays were performed in bright costumes and on the back of huge carts called **pageants**.

Elizabethan theatre

Secular plays, in a tradition going back to Roman times at least, were performed in public spaces, and, increasingly, in the courtyards of inns, where the audience could watch from the yard itself or could look down at the action from the corridors that ran on each storey around the yard. From this tradition the Elizabethan theatre emerged, with its characteristic **thrust stage**, bringing the actors right out into the audience, many of whom stood at their feet. The Globe theatre on the south bank of the Thames in London is a reconstruction of such an Elizabethan theatre.

The arrows, here as in the diagrams that follow, indicate the direction of the audience's gaze when watching the action.

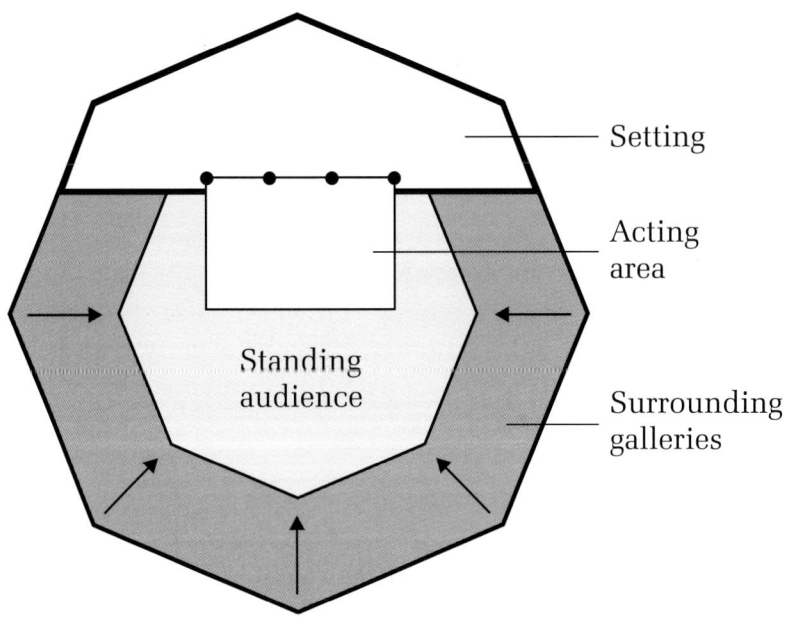

An Elizabethan public theatre

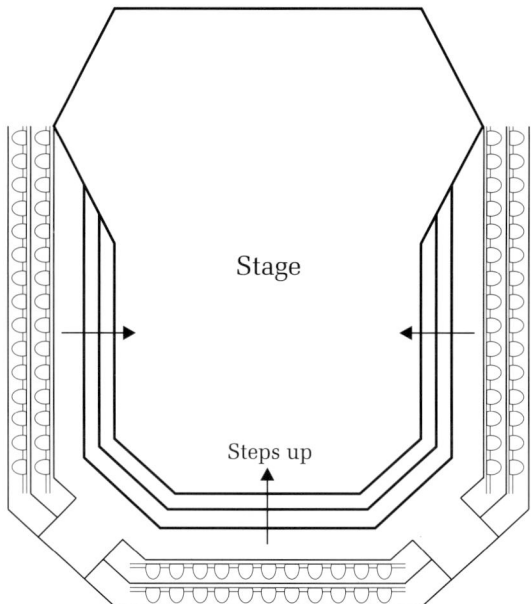

A thrust stage

At this time, rich aristocrats often commissioned plays to be performed privately for themselves and their guests. These plays would be acted out in halls, such as those that survive in the colleges of Oxford and Cambridge and elsewhere. From this tradition, rather than the open-air tradition of the Globe, the theatre of the 17th and 18th centuries emerged: the **end-on theatre**, where the stage is at one of the short ends of a rectangle and the audience occupies the body of the rectangle and perhaps vantage points on the three facing walls.

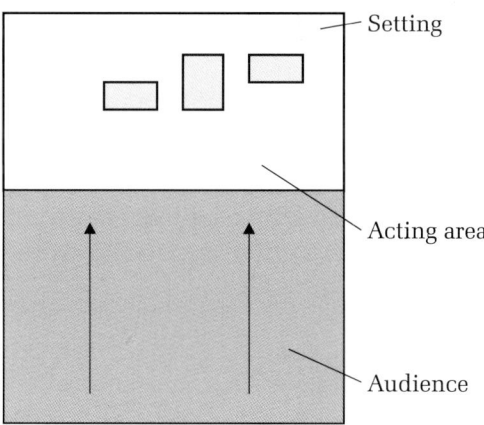

An end-on stage

End-on theatre

Web link

At least two important theatres from the end of this period survive in England: the Georgian Theatre Royal in Richmond, Yorkshire, built in 1788 (www.georgiantheatreroyal.co.uk) and the Theatre Royal in Bury St Edmund's, opened in 1819 (www.theatreroyal.org).

As theatres grew in size, so the performing area grew more distinct from the audience, and the **proscenium arch** was built to frame the performers, so that the audience watched the show through the arch, which was closed with a curtain for scene changes and at the end of acts. The curtains which close across the proscenium arch are called **house tabs**. The **apron** of the stage is that section which protrudes in front of the proscenium arch. In plays from the 18th and 19th century, you can often see how dramatists structured their plays to take advantage of this system. Relatively long and detailed scenes taking place in clear settings such as living rooms or salons are alternated with exterior scenes which take place in the street and involve fewer characters or less action. This is to

Proscenium arch

Sheridan's play *The Rivals* works well in this way, using such devices and the ends of acts to allow time for scene changes.

allow a painted curtain to cover the stage area, while characters meet on the 'street' along the apron of the stage; when that scene is over, the curtain is drawn to reveal another carefully assembled interior.

Acts and scenes

In these terms, a **scene** is a practical division of the play into episodes, while an **act** is an artistic division revealing the structure of the play. It was traditional for people to take refreshment between the acts, and in some theatres of this period (and later), where the wealthy and the fashionable met, this socialising became more important than the play itself.

Modern staging

Modern theatre design tends to be flexible, so that performances can be given in ways that echo one or more of these more historical styles. As a result, other styles of staging have emerged:

➤ A **traverse stage** is one which runs between two auditorium areas, enabling action to sweep along it

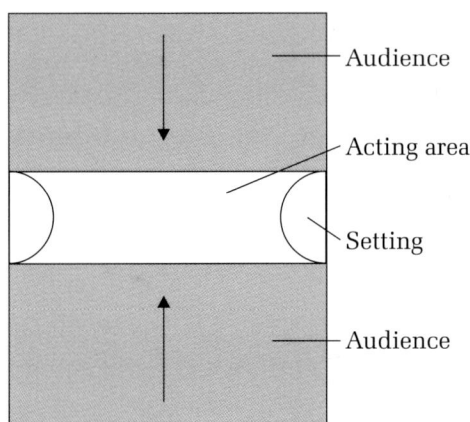

A traverse stage

➤ A **promenade production** is one where the actors mingle with the audience, who have to walk around or 'promenade' in order to follow the action

➤ **Theatre in the round** is performed from a central stage with the auditorium like a doughnut around the outside, in a way reminiscent of an amphitheatre.

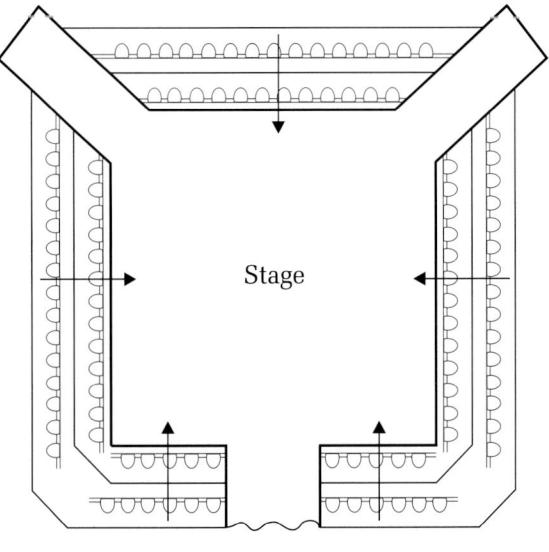

A theatre in the round

Modern directors are often free to adapt their performance space to suit the vision they have for the play that they are directing; each of these staging designs creates a different relationship between players and audience and different patterns of movement.

A lot of the specialist vocabulary for describing the practical elements of a theatre derives from the proscenium arch theatres of the 18th century. In those days, the stage was often **raked**, so that the back, furthest from the audience, was raised a little. This enabled everyone to be able to see the action. As a result the back of the stage in this sense is still called **upstage** and the front **downstage**. The terms **stage left** and **stage right** refer to the actor's left and right as they face the auditorium, which can be confusing!

Stage designers introduced features on the stage to create **levels**, which meant some actors could be higher than others, creating visual interest and some symbolic effect. It was also traditional to design a set with a significant **backdrop** upstage. In provincial theatres, where these existed, there was simply a collection of such backdrops and the most appropriate were chosen and used; in London, gifted artists painted them. The **melodramas** of the 19th century – big, sentimental narrative plays – used incredibly effective and sophisticated backdrops.

Many modern productions dispense with backdrops. Often they are replaced by a **cyclorama**, a blank surface, cleverly or significantly lit, which runs behind the performing space. In some modern productions, the cyclorama is used as a screen for projected digital images.

Upstage, downstage

Directors use this terminology when working on the blocking of a play with actors, allowing them to give simple instructions to the actors as to where they should move.

Levels and backdrops

A backdrop is a large cloth on which a realistic image is painted to suggest a location for a scene. These days backdrops are most commonly seen in pantomimes, where quick scene changes are required.

When touring companies are arranging their schedules, their managers need full details of the stages and theatres where they are to perform. Theatres provide detailed descriptions of their facilities. This is an extract from the details provided by one such theatre: you should be able to understand it all now!

> Wokingham Theatre has a stage area approximately 28' wide, 23' deep and 14' high. The apron protrudes 5' and extends stage right by another 4'.
>
> Stage left wing space is 9' by 23' and has the stage manager's desk behind the proscenium arch. Stage right is, again, 9' wide and 23' deep. There is a walkway behind the cyclorama wall to allow access to both sides of the stage. This wall is 34' wide and extends to full height. There is also a white cyclorama screen that covers the whole wall.

The stage manager has overall control of the performance and is responsible for signalling the cues that coordinate the work of the actors and technicians. Once the director has left the production (often after the first night) the stage manager is the most important person on a production.

Set

In Elizabethan times, there was little or no set in the theatre. As the years passed, however, designers began to pay more and more attention to designing the stage to suit the action taking place on it. They would use **stage plans** to ensure that their designs were practicable and allowed the plays to be performed. Often this included making models of the set to show what was required and how things would work.

Stage plans

If you choose to assume the role of designer when working on your devised piece, you will need to submit such a model of your set. See page 28.

Flats

Where flats are stationary, as in a traditional box set, they are held in place through a system of weights and braces.

Flats are painted scenery panels that are used to create different kinds of space on stage. Some of these are hung from the space at the top of the stage (the **flies**) and are called **flown scenery**; others may be fixed on wheels or **trucks** to enable movement. Some designers, especially during the 19th century when realism became fashionable, worked very hard to create **perspective** on stage. In some European productions, the designer even employed people of short stature to fill out the crowd upstage, so as to add to effects of perspective!

Effects

Sometimes such scenery was extremely ambitious, a heritage which survives in the traditional West End productions in which big stage effects are often celebrated as ends in themselves. **Hydraulics** may be used to raise or lower whole areas of the stage in order to create such big effects; a **rain curtain** may be used to create the effect of rainfall, by supplying a narrow shower of water which is collected in guttering and recycled (rarely without spillage and complications!) Sometimes, stages may **revolve**, allowing intricate scenery to change within minutes. Such productions often use a wealth of special effects.

Lighting

There was, of course, little or no lighting in the theatre until relatively modern times – although it's worth remembering that it was a **pyrotechnic** (or firework) effect, designed to make the firing of a cannon more realistic, which led to the burning down of Shakespeare's Globe in 1613 – but now complex lighting is a key part in even the smallest production.

The **lighting plot** is the term given to the way the play is lit from beginning to end. The lighting designer must first arrange and focus the lanterns to create the **lighting rig** for this particular production. This will include the use of colour **gels** to create specific effects, and of **gobos**, which are metal silhouettes placed in front of a lantern's lens so that shadows of a specific design are cast on the stage. In this way, a lighting designer can create the effects of moonlit windows, the dappled light of a forest and so on. Many students underestimate the importance of the lighting rig, and of colouring and focusing the light they are going to use. It is wise not to do so.

Lanterns

If you are studying Craig as your practitioner, you will need to know that he was keen on the use of such effects in his designs. See page 134.

The lanterns can be shining from above the auditorium, perhaps from one of the higher levels of seating or from the side of the stage. Often they are held on a **gantry** which suspends them above the auditorium or above the stage itself. By varying the angle of the light beams, a lighting designer can create interesting and atmospheric visual effects. **Chiaroscuro** is an artistic term used to refer to an image that is dramatically lit in order to provide some brightly lit surfaces and some deep shadow.

There is a whole range of terms to describe the different lanterns available to a lighting designer, and only the most common are glossed here:

➤ A **flood** provides a bland, unfocused light and, although popular, is the least useful stage lantern

➤ A **fresnel** lantern is much more versatile, using a special lens to create a spotlight effect

> A **profile** uses a different kind of lens to produce a sharp, narrow beam of light

> A **parcan** is a type of lantern which projects a light that is bright but unfocused and in an oval or elliptical shape

> A **birdie** is a small parcan used to light awkward corners of a set, or to be placed on the front of a stage to uplight faces and create interesting shadows on the cyclorama

> A **strobe** emits a regular series of high power flashes (which can provoke epileptic fits in some individuals, hence warnings must be published in the theatre if a strobe light is to be used).

Lighting effects can be enhanced by the use of **gauze**, which is a coarsely woven cloth. When lit from the front, it is opaque; when lit from behind it becomes transparent. The effect is similar to net curtains in a house.

Sound

Just as a lighting plot contributes to the overall design of a play, so does a **soundscape**. This is where a collage of sound effects and music can create a kind of aural backdrop to some or all of the action.

It is important to remember that none of this design work should overshadow the role in a performance of the actor, whose speech and gestures communicate the play to the audience. In creating a character, an actor will use voice and body. Some playwrights, such as William Congreve, were famous in their day for creating distinctive 'voices' for their characters. A good actor will be sensitive to the **diction** or the choice of words given to a character. By finding an appropriate **accent** and **pitch**, a good actor can create a convincing speech pattern for a character.

> Congreve (1670–1729) is considered one of the best comic dramatists of the restoration period. See page 67 for more on accent and pitch.

Drama theory and analysis

Origins of Greek theatre

It will be helpful to you to know some of the key developments in the history of theatre and performance. Greek theatre is an obvious starting point. Greek theatre began at a festival held each spring in honour of Dionysus, the god of wine, youth and fertility. He was also a spirit of energy, action and violence, and a bringer of madness. Dionysus was the son of Zeus (a god) and Semele (a mortal). Semele was killed before Dionysus was born so Zeus took the baby from her body and planted it in his thigh. Later, Dionysus was born from Zeus' thigh – thus he was twice born. The hymn sung to Dionysus by his followers is the dithyramb, which means 'twice born'. Dionysus was a god of possession; he could reveal himself to his followers directly while they were in a state of *ecstasis* (trance). Worship was liberating for them and freed them from the constraints of society. This was directly opposite to the ordered Greek society, which was politically and socially sophisticated, aware of its own identity and proud of it. By worshipping Dionysus, the individual was allowed to question the very nature of society. This explains why the start of theatre in Greek society was so explosive: it jolted the audience into questioning the nature of their own existence, something that all good theatre has done ever since. Greek drama asks questions of its audience, it seeks out the irrational in society and in the destiny of man. It demands that the audience experience that which cannot be rationalised. It does not provide the answers – the individual must do that for themselves – but it provides the experiences to allow the right questions to be asked. At the very centre of Greek drama is the conflict between man and god.

Dramatic festivals

The festival in Athens was a competition for performances of tragic plays with three performed each day (followed by a lighter satyr play to round off the day). The word tragedy comes from 'tragoidia' meaning 'goat song', probably because a goat was originally given as a prize or sacrifice. Thespis, who is seen as the father of the theatre and after whom actors are named today (thespians), won this play competition in 534 BCE. It is thought that he was the first 'actor' to step forward from the chorus and take on one of the characters of the story. As the drama evolved Aeschylus (525–456 BCE) added a second actor, which allowed for greater conflict and plot, and then Sophocles (496–406 BCE) added a third, which enabled him to humanise the dialogue still further and to develop interplay between the actors. The chorus members were now used as witnesses and as lyrical commentators on the action, becoming the link between the audience and the play, asking the questions the audience should be asking of themselves. The dramatic conflict becomes one that seemingly has right on both sides and, when no compromise is given, must end in disaster for both sides.

Aristotle and tragedy

'Jacobean' refers to the age of James I of England, VI of Scotland (reigned in England 1603–1625).

The ancient Greek philosopher Aristotle (384–322 BCE) explored the genre of tragedy in his work of literary criticism, the *Poetics*. His discussion was hugely influential on the tragedies of the Elizabethan and Jacobean ages. Aristotle thought that a tragedy should involve a protagonist of high estate who falls from prosperity to misery through a series of discoveries, as the result of a tragic flaw which is usually based on moral or human weakness. According to Aristotle, the action of the play should include:

➤ **Revolution**: the unanticipated reversal of what is expected to occur

➤ **Discovery**: a turning point in the play when the protagonist and the audience learn something that had previously been hidden

➤ **Disasters**: here all the destructive actions and deaths occur.

Aristotle thought that to be tragedy, a play should invoke pity and fear in the audience. He suggested that this allowed the audience to find a kind of release from their own pent-up emotions in seeing similar emotions exaggerated to breaking-point in performance. He called this release **catharsis**.

Development of drama

As theatre developed in Europe – from classical times, through the medieval and renaissance periods, the Age of Enlightenment and the 19th century, to the developments of the 20th century – so the style of play and the style of performance also developed.

Shakespeare mocks this kind of classification of plays in his own *A Midsummer Night's Dream*.

Following the prominence of religious plays in medieval times, the renaissance in western Europe rediscovered the ancient play-texts, and playwrights once again became explicitly interested in writing comedy and tragedy. They also explored mixing the styles, producing plays with tragic openings and happy endings; people call such plays **tragi-comedies**.

The Elizabethan period (1558–1603) or late renaissance – the era in which Shakespeare came to prominence in England (and Lope de Vega and Cervantes in Spain) – provided very little scenery or effects in its theatres. Instead, the job was done by verbal imagery. Sometimes – in a modern production with a full set and design plan, or in a film, for example – Shakespeare's language can seem slow and redundant, for all its beauty. But his poetic imagery was feeding the imagination of his audience; he needed to remind them over and over again that Romeo and Juliet were meeting at night, because his play was being performed under an afternoon sky. In a modern theatre, where the lights are dimmed and dark shadows fill the stage, this repetition can seem to slow the play down, but in its original context, it was vitally necessary.

Verbal imagery

Many of these plays were written in verse. This has many merits, but an important one – often neglected or undervalued – concerns the ease with which a rhythmic line can be **projected** by the actor's voice. Getting the words of *Hamlet* across audibly in a Shakespearean theatre was made much easier by giving each line a rhythmic balance and pulse. In English, the **iambic pentameter** (five stressed syllables alternating with five unstressed ones) turned out to be perfect for this.

Rhythm

The Jacobean period in England, and the baroque period on the continent, witnessed the further polarisation of the two genres of tragedy and comedy. In England, Jacobean tragedy is notorious for its violence and cruelty; but some comedies embraced the values of the court **masque**, which was almost performance for performance's sake. Similar extravagances are found in European plays of this period, including those from the 'Golden Age' in Spain by playwrights such as Calderón de la Barca and Tirso de Molina.

The baroque period was the 17th and early 18th century. Its literature, art and music often explored rich, ornate effects and celebrated extremes.

The European comedy of the late 17th and 18th century was essentially sexual in theme, dealing with the relationships between men and women among the relaxed and decadent mores of the moneyed classes. The stage now had actresses – up until this point, women's parts had been played by boys – and playwrights took every advantage of this change. These plays, often called **restoration comedies** in England (where Charles II had been restored to the throne in 1660) were almost always **comedies of manners**, mocking the values of the audience that had come to watch, but at the same time rather celebrating them. Such a style remained popular throughout the Georgian period, too. These plays were often set in interiors and performed in intimate theatres, as we have seen. Therefore, they lent themselves to the use of prose in their speeches. However, this prose was not a true reflection of the way people naturally spoke at this time: it was still carefully poised and artfully balanced, to emphasise the wit of the language and the ideas. It is not, in the end, very much more realistic than verse.

Restoration comedies

Examples include William Wycherley's *The Country Wife* and *The Plain Dealer*, as well as Congreve's *Love for Love* and *The Way of the World*.

'Georgian' refers to the period of the reigns of the four Georges (and one William!), from 1714 to 1830.

Realism

During the 19th century, though, there developed a much greater emphasis on **realism**, making things look and sound as they do in real life. Many theatre companies spent enormous amounts of time and money creating the realistic appearance of the play's setting. Gerhardt Hauptmann's play *The Weavers* is just one of a number of

Hauptmann (1862–1946) was a prominent German dramatist who won the Nobel prize for literature in 1912. *The Weavers* (1893) is one of his best known works. For more on Ibsen and realism, see page 56.

plays from this period that require very complex and detailed settings. Other playwrights, though, demanded a simpler kind of realism. The plays of Henrik Ibsen (1828–1906), for example, demand accurate Scandinavian interiors.

Stock characters

The result of this movement towards realism was the need for a fundamentally different kind of acting. The comedies of manners of the 18th and 19th centuries relied on **stock characters** and **stock situations**. Actors used **stock gestures** – clasping their hands to their breast, for example, at moments of high passion – and played in clothes they liked, rather than in costumes that suited their characters.

Commedia dell'arte

In some ways, this style of acting was part of a tradition that dated back to the **commedia dell'arte** of the late Italian renaissance, which came to have an important influence on theatre throughout Europe. As performers of commedia used stock masks to represent their characters, this led to a very physical style of exaggerated comic acting. Commedia plays were largely improvised in public places, and their plots involved the interaction of a group of stock characters, including the beautiful young woman Columbina and the greedy merchant Pantalone. Wit, topicality and physical humour were important elements of the commedia.

Stanislavski

See page 124 for more on this.

This kind of approach did not suit a realistic writer like Ibsen or Chekhov and ran counter to their aims. A significant change in acting style was now essential. In the end, the work of the Russian director Stanislavski represented this revolution in acting. He saw that realism worked through **metonymy**, which is the suggestion of a whole through the revelation just of parts. He devised a series of approaches to the text that allowed the actors to explore the devices of metonymy used in the play, so that they could create psychologically realistic characters. Many terms from Stanislavski's writing have entered into general use in the theatre, and are explained in detail in the large section on his work on pages 102–117.

Naturalism

Growing out of realism, **naturalism** was a philosophical approach to life that derived from Charles Darwin's work in biology. Naturalist writers, such as Zola in France, Ibsen in Norway and Thomas Hardy in England, followed Darwin's view that people (or species) were created by a combination of heredity and environment. Their writings placed great emphasis on parentage and on location in exploring character and motive.

In this way, naturalist plays often exemplify the values of the well-made play as defined by the prolific French writer Eugene Scribe.

Naturalist plays usually present a tense situation, whereby one small intervention from outside will strain things to breaking point. The play describes the situation, the intervention, the tension, the breaking point and the aftermath. They use realism to emphasise their naturalism, presenting their intimate scenes in realistic settings, so that it is as if the 'fourth wall' of the room has been peeled away allowing the audience to peer in.

Metaphor

Inevitably, dramatists began to enjoy the effects of exploring the kind of deep, repressed emotion which the naturalists were tapping into. The **expressionist** writers of the early 20th century articulated often extreme emotion and dramatised it through symbol and metaphor. Sometimes, this metaphor went well beyond reality and became **surreal**, like the imagery of dreams and the art of the Surrealists, or **absurd**. Actors in such plays often had to be athletic and able to discover profound emotions on stage, as Artaud recognised. This preference for metaphor over metonymy was a characteristic of the **modernist** movement. Metonymy shows what something looks like: metaphor reveals what it is, modernists might say.

Other playwrights rejected this extremism and wrote **symbolist** plays, whose meanings were less precise, hinted at with imagery that was often visual or musical, rather than explicit. The verse plays of W. B. Yeats are typical of symbolist drama.

By the second half of the 20th century, theatre had become rich and varied: former styles of writing and performing, including a continued interest in putting on **period plays** (old plays in the style associated with them), were existing side by side with more experimental work. **Political theatre** set out to alert the audience to social and economic issues, using populist techniques such as song, as well as **polemic** – politically explicit persuasive language. **Physical theatre** moved away from the power of the written script to embrace movement and dance elements. **Community theatre** valued the cooperation of a community in a production more than professionalism and perfection in performance.

Symbolism

See pages 117–128 for more on Artaud.

Further study

Find out what the expression 'agit prop' means and think how it might be used in a theatrical context.

Understanding the text

Identifying forms and characters

When writing about a play, we need to use some specialist vocabulary in order to make our comments precise and specific. Obviously, we are already able to use terms such as **character** and **role**, but there are other aspects of characterisation that you will need to be able to identify and label. When identifying the main character in the play – if there is one – you can refer to them as the **hero**, even if they don't do anything very heroic. Another term that you might prefer is **protagonist**, which draws attention to the fact that your character instigates the action. Then you might call the key character whose life is affected as a result of the action of the protagonist, the **antagonist**. When the hero is actually nothing like a hero, but displays characteristics which are in fact pretty negative or despicable, you can refer to them as the **anti-hero**.

You may find that when characters first appear, the playwright suggests certain **stereotypical** features about them, so that we can recognise quickly what kind of people they are. Usually, as the play develops, these stereotypical features are modified and made more interesting.

When looking at a script, you may need to identify a number of different forms or structures. A **monologue**, for example, is a fairly long, significant speech delivered by one character. Sometimes a monologue is delivered to other characters on stage. If it is delivered to the audience alone, it has a specific name, a **soliloquy**. A **duologue** is a name for a section of text where two characters speak to one another; **dialogue** is the term for any section of conversation

Characters

When talking about all the roles in a play, you can use the Latin term **dramatis personae**, which in English translates as 'the people of the play'.

Forms

involving two or more characters. An **aside** is a rather artificial device whereby an actor comments directly to the audience, apparently unheard by the other actors.

Features

We can also analyse features of the text. The **plot**, of course, is the sequence of events that structure the play; the **subplot** is a second, subordinate section of the story that almost stands on its own, and which complements the main plot – either by repeating some of its themes though handling them differently (as in *King Lear*) or by developing contrasting ones (as in *Twelfth Night*). When a subplot provides a humorous element that contrasts with the serious main plot, we may call this an example of **comic relief**.

You might also want to structure your thoughts about the whole play or each individual scene by locating within it certain elements of basic narrative. For example, first there is a **situation**, explained by an initial **exposition**. This is in due course interrupted by a **complication**. (Sometimes this leads to a whole series of **advances** and **reversals**.) This then leads to a **crisis** and then to a **climax**. After the climax there is a **resolution** or a **denouement**, which ends the play or scene.

Sometimes, the denouement may feel rather contrived. In many Greek plays, when the situation within the play had become very complicated, an actor representing a god appeared, suspended from some sort of crane, to resolve everything. A phrase emerged from this: **deus ex machina**. This Latin phrase means 'a god from a machine', but now it is used to mean any sudden, rather unconvincing conclusion. For example, a letter might arrive that somehow sorts out a complicated situation quickly, but unconvincingly.

Style and genre

One key challenge facing a performer, a director or a designer when confronted by a new or unfamiliar text is to identify both genre and style. This will help them understand how its meanings are to be conveyed. It's thus probably helpful to be clear about the difference between **genre** and **style**. Genre describes the kind of play we are dealing with: words that describe genre include tragedy, comedy, **satire** and **melodrama**. Some genre terms are more specific than others (melodrama, for example, relates to a very specific type of play), some, like tragedy, have provoked debate and some controversy and can refer to a large variety of plays.

Style refers to the options chosen by a director when presenting the play on stage, which includes both the manner of performance and the production elements such as setting and costume design. In other words a comedy (genre) might be presented on stage in the style of a pantomime or in the style of physical theatre. Style can also relate more directly to the historical period in which a play was first produced, so that when we say that *A Midsummer Night's Dream* is performed in a Shakespearean style, we will be expecting a classically Elizabethan production. However, a director might choose to present the play out of its historical style, to reveal other levels of meaning. When we go to see a production of a familiar play, what interests us is often no longer the story but the new

Exposition is where characters reveal their 'back-story', the important background information about themselves or the situation they are in.

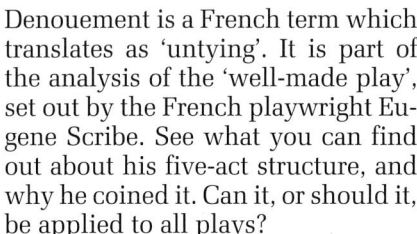

Further study

Denouement is a French term which translates as 'untying'. It is part of the analysis of the 'well-made play', set out by the French playwright Eugene Scribe. See what you can find out about his five-act structure, and why he coined it. Can it, or should it, be applied to all plays?

interpretation, which invites us to revisit the text and see something new in it.

Spotting the features of style in a play, therefore, requires experience and wider reading. The type of language, for example, will help us identify the style of performance. Can a verse play be played realistically? Can a play full of witty jokes be expected to move its audience to tears? How has the writer hinted at voice and tone? As a director should you always follow the style of the writing when deciding how to present your production, or can it be advantageous to go against the written style to make a particular point to your audience?

Subtext

People don't always say what they mean. In our ordinary lives, we can feel insulted by silence. Playwrights (and actors) love this. When we read a new scene, we can ask ourselves, do these people mean exactly what they say, or are they hinting at something else? This hidden message – the **subtext** – provides great interest for us all. A lot of the enjoyment an audience gets in the theatre concerns the use of subtext. When characters don't say what they mean, or give away what they're feeling by saying something improbable, the audience loves to solve the problem and to work out exactly what it is that makes these characters tick.

Dramatic intention

By looking at a text in this way we can begin to ask ourselves what the writer's **dramatic intention** is. Do not think of a play as a novel written for the stage. A playwright uses all of the stage's potential to create their meanings. Silent characters, small props, the painted view out of a small window: all these contribute to dramatic effect, so be sensitive to them.

After you have read a text, you will be able to understand something about its **theme**, the abstract or intellectual idea behind the drama. In a realistic drama we tend to see the action as being part of a bigger social issue; in a more poetic drama, it is up to us to interpret the action and find the deeper meaning. Playwrights often use **symbolism** to help create meaning and develop themes: it is one of their most powerful tools, allowing them to use seemingly ordinary events and actions to highlight a more significant issue. For example, if you see someone eating an apple in the auditorium you might rightly just assume they are having a snack: if you see someone eating an apple on stage, it could be reference to Adam and Eve, and thus to all sorts of themes such as the nature of sin, creation and so on.

Sometimes, scenes in a play offer a kind of simplified version of a complex issue. By creating such an **analogy**, the playwright is able to create more meaning. Sometimes, the analogy is so overarching that the whole play works on a completely different level: then it becomes an **allegory**. The characters in an allegory sometimes have no individual personality at all, but simply embody the issues or moral qualities involved.

David Edgar's play *Pentecost* begins with a Balkan art expert removing bricks from the back wall of an old church so that she can show a visiting English art professor a remarkable medieval painting. This can be interpreted as a symbol for the cultural heritage running behind the problems in the Balkans; the relationship between the woman and the man seems to have something of an allegory about it, replicating perhaps the relationship between the Balkans and the West. In this way, one of Edgar's dramatic intentions – that of alerting his audience to the political issues of the Balkans – is already clear after the first few minutes.

Audience reaction

When we read a text like Edgar's, therefore, we are already beginning to form an interpretation of it, based on our understanding of the intentions we read behind the writing. We balance a whole range of different signals: language, stage action, characters, gesture and so on, to create our own reading of the play.

However, the final summing up of an interpretation concerns the audience: how do we want them to respond? Do we want them just want to be entertained? Do we want them to be horrified, to experience some sort of catharsis? Do we want them to laugh at one another, or themselves? Do we want them to think about something? This final interpretation needs to be mapped on to the text. You must guard against jumping to quick conclusions about a character or about the function of a speech and then forcing other elements of a text into line with these initial misconceptions. Keep testing your ideas against the text so that your conclusions are water-tight.

Devised Drama

What have I got to do?

For this part of your AS-level course, you have to do the following things:

➤ You've got to produce an original piece of theatre that stands on its own and that makes appropriate demands of its audience.

➤ You must prepare, develop and present this piece as part of a group. To be successful, there must be a real sense of creative cooperation throughout this process. However, you must choose a particular performance skill that you personally will demonstrate. This can be acting, but it can also be any one of the following design skills: costume design and construction; stage design; mask design; lighting and/or sound design. You must demonstrate your knowledge and understanding of these skills, your ability to employ them, and your readiness to experiment with them to develop and improve them.

➤ You have to record your work in a portfolio, which will be assessed along with the standard of your preparatory work and the standard of the final performance.

Your piece must be clearly related in some way to one of the set texts you are reading; to the practitioners whose work you are studying; or to one of the productions you have seen during the course. It must be technically accomplished and professionally presented.

This part of the course requires a minimum of eight weeks' work. We recommend that you read through all the following sections before starting, and then revisit them when you need to during your preparation and rehearsal period.

The portfolio

A quarter of the marks for this module are reserved for the personal portfolio. The golden rule for achieving a high mark for your portfolio is to manage it from day one. Retrospective portfolios – scribbled down during the last possible few days when you should be concentrating on your performance – will inevitably gain low marks as well as distracting you from your performing. Use the portfolio as a notebook, a diary, a series of experimental jottings. Make it interesting rather than polished, exploratory rather than conclusive, a collage rather than a painting. It should be a sketchbook for the finished work, which will be the performance. In these ways, it will document the work in progress.

In the course of completing this work, you will outline your own role in the development of the performance piece. If you find one day that you have too little to add to your portfolio, maybe this is because you are contributing too little to the group's work. Think about this.

Acting

If you are focusing on acting in the final piece, you should give details of your approach to performance skills, and you should also describe your experiments with techniques and the work you've done to build a character. (There are hints about how you might go about doing this in the following pages.) What research have you undertaken? What skills have you had to work on? What rehearsal techniques have you used? What advice have you been given? How useful was it? How have the ideas from your theory modules helped you here?

Designing

If you intend to be assessed as a designer for the final piece, your portfolio should include relevant sketches, diagrams and photographs. If you decide to focus on costume design, you may wish to include samples of materials or dyes used; if you focus on stage settings you will need to produce a scale model of the set for the group piece. Lighting and sound designers must include lists of the equipment and accessories used, as well as things like cue sheets and plot sheets. Whatever aspect of design you look at, you'll need to be able to include a personal evaluation of the creative cooperation of the group as well as self-assessment. You'll evaluate the successful development of the project against the original aims. You will have developed and modified your design proposals as the project grows, and you will relate these changes to the original concept. You also need to show a thorough awareness of health and safety factors and their implications for your work.

The examiners advise you that although there is no prescribed format for the portfolio, it should be written in an appropriate tone, using specialist terminology where appropriate. It should be approximately 2,000 words in length. Do not waste time counting words – use your time to develop ideas and then record them in your portfolio – but remember that great length does not necessarily equal great quality. Your portfolio should be relevant and well organised.

The portfolio should be a working book, but it should be legible and logical, of course, because someone else has to read it. It should offer an insight into your thoughts and ideas as the original piece progresses. It should show that the final piece of theatre is the result of intellectual rigour and artistic sensitivity, and not just a collection of dodgy audition pieces put together by instinct and luck.

High-grade portfolios

The examination board has published some guidance concerning the qualities of a first-rate portfolio. It is useful to unpick their instructions and see exactly what they mean:

66 **The dramatic aims and objectives of the group will be precisely defined.** 99

Your aims are the big and abstract ideas behind the piece you produce. Maybe you want to confront the audience with a tragic dilemma; maybe you want to explore the effect of a tragic accident on a family or depict the effect of a big social change on a small community; maybe you want to show the spiritual journey of a young man.

Your objectives are smaller. You may want to: entertain your audience by creating realistic dialogue and psychologically convincing characters; puzzle them with shocking and violent images; or amuse them with humour and humorous situations.

You'll notice that the question 'why' is still lurking under these aims and objectives. It's a question worth asking. Why do you want to confront the audience with a tragic dilemma? For their own good? In order for you to have a better idea about the function of tragedy? In order for you and the audience to understand the genre of tragedy better? By asking such questions you will be able to clarify your aims and refine your objectives. You'll find out, if you do this bit of thinking clearly, that when you look at your objectives and ask why, you'll find yourself going back to the aims.

You'll also see that the aims will be abstract and intellectual, whereas the objectives will be practical and concrete. Use your portfolio to make notes, because thinking about your aims and objectives cannot really be finished at the first discussion. As you undertake research and experimentation, you'll find yourselves amending your objectives, even if your aims remain firm.

> **The whole process of preparation will be clearly and purposefully documented and analysed in the candidate's personal portfolio, which will contain evidence of the candidate's pursuit of excellence in shaping his/her own contribution, as performer or designer, to the dramatic intentions of the group in the preparation of the piece for performance.**

The 'pursuit of excellence' – that phrase is a key one, isn't it? Your portfolio should naturally describe what you've done, but it should also contain your thoughts on how to make it better, how to achieve your objectives as effectively and as purely as possible. You can also see the importance of completing the portfolio as you go along, recording the pursuit, not – to continue the metaphor – just the kill.

> **Candidates will define their inspiration for the piece from the AS Subject Content with precision and enthusiasm, demonstrating a clear commitment to the chosen dramatic form, style or practitioner. The portfolio will contain evidence of a judicious approach to research and a successful application of the fruits of that research to the group aims.**

If you do not think that the demand to link the theme or form of your original piece to something you have met elsewhere in the AS course is a limitation, then you have not understood the requirement. It is a limitation. You must work on an area which is related to your study of a set text or of a practitioner. If you do not feel limited in some way by this requirement, you may not be fulfilling it. Be careful.

On the other hand, if you feel creatively hamstrung by this requirement, then you have not understood the generosity of the word 'inspiration'. Set texts have a huge frame of reference and you can choose to develop just one part of this. O'Casey's plays deal with Irish politics, of course, but they also deal with tensions within tight communities, and they deal with contemporary issues

Design factors

♦ A clear idea about aims and objectives is just as important for the design of your piece as it is for its content and style. Different stage layouts create different relationships with the audience, for example. How do your aims affect the relationship between performers and audience? How will your choice of staging contribute to achieving this aim?

♦ The use of masks also influences audience response, and makes a significant contribution to mood and atmosphere, as well as helping to define genre. Have you considered using them?

♦ Do you have a designer in your team who will lead in these areas, or will the group be sharing responsibility?

Design factors

Different genres require different styles of acting and different accents on design. As you clarify the shape and form of your piece, you must clarify how the design of it will contribute to its effect.

in an almost documentary style. They use realistic speech patterns and they employ realistic sets. Any one of these elements could be a starting point for work of your own. In plays like *Yerma* Lorca writes about Andalusia in particular, but he also evokes a rural lifestyle, explores the tensions in an adult sexual relationship, mingles verse and prose, and uses ritual and chorus in a realistic setting. Again, any of these elements can be a starting point for your own work. Artaud stresses the importance of ritual and of finding a new language for the theatre; Stanislavski wants to communicate reality through a few exactly-drawn sweeps of a brush; Craig wants the audience to lose themselves in a largely symbolic and beautiful world. There's plenty here to build on! Make sure you outline your influences carefully in your portfolio, demonstrating the role they played throughout the devising process.

> ❝ **All the material within the portfolio will be directly relevant to the candidate's engagement with the developing piece. The portfolio will reveal that the candidate has a clear understanding of his/her own strengths and weaknesses as well as an appreciation of the relative merits of the piece as a whole. The portfolio will demonstrate meticulous concern for health and safety factors.** ❞

Although your portfolio should offer more than just a diary, there is a diary element to it and that element should enable you to engage with the developing piece. It will show your understanding of what you are doing well, where you are meeting your own personal objectives, and where you are not quite succeeding. Be objective about your successes and honest about your limitations. That will help you feel good about what you can do and also help you to focus on areas where things aren't perfect, where you can seek advice or undertake further exploration.

> ❝ **The portfolio will be presented logically and will be well written in an appropriate register using specialist terminology accurately and with confidence.** ❞

'An appropriate register' is a flexible phrase. A portfolio is not a polished essay. But it isn't a series of illegible jottings either. The following suggestions should help you to see how to write up your day's work, and how to make your notes and speculations readable:

➢ Don't be afraid to write questions as well as answers. Often, improving your ability to ask the right question is the easiest way to finding the best answer.

➢ You are an actor; you are a designer; you are a director. You are no longer a student. You should adopt the language of the theatre and the concepts of the theatre. Your portfolio should be as professional a piece of work as you can possibly make it.

➢ It's really useful to think of your portfolio as a notebook, as a sketchbook. So buy a really decent notebook or an artist's sketchbook to use. Visit the art department in your school or college and look at the ways in which the art students use their sketchbooks to prepare for their own examination pieces. That's what you should be doing in your portfolio.

'An appropriate register' is like saying, 'in a suitable tone of voice'. It means the style is right.

A4 artist's sketchbooks are not cheap, but they are worth every penny. They feel good to use, the paper is excellent, and there is a real sense of accomplishment in using one.

➤ Using such a sketchbook can make you very versatile. If you make jottings during a rehearsal, glue them in. Add a comment or two. You might find a photograph in a magazine or newspaper, or a postcard at an art gallery, that somehow sums up just the mood or image you're after: glue it in with a comment. You might have a series of digital photographs from a research visit or a rehearsal – stick them in with a commentary. The final product should be informative, coherent and easily understood by an outsider, but it should also be creative and fun. The following is a double-page spread taken from a portfolio. Remember that this is an example to stimulate your own creativity, it's not here as a model for you to follow slavishly.

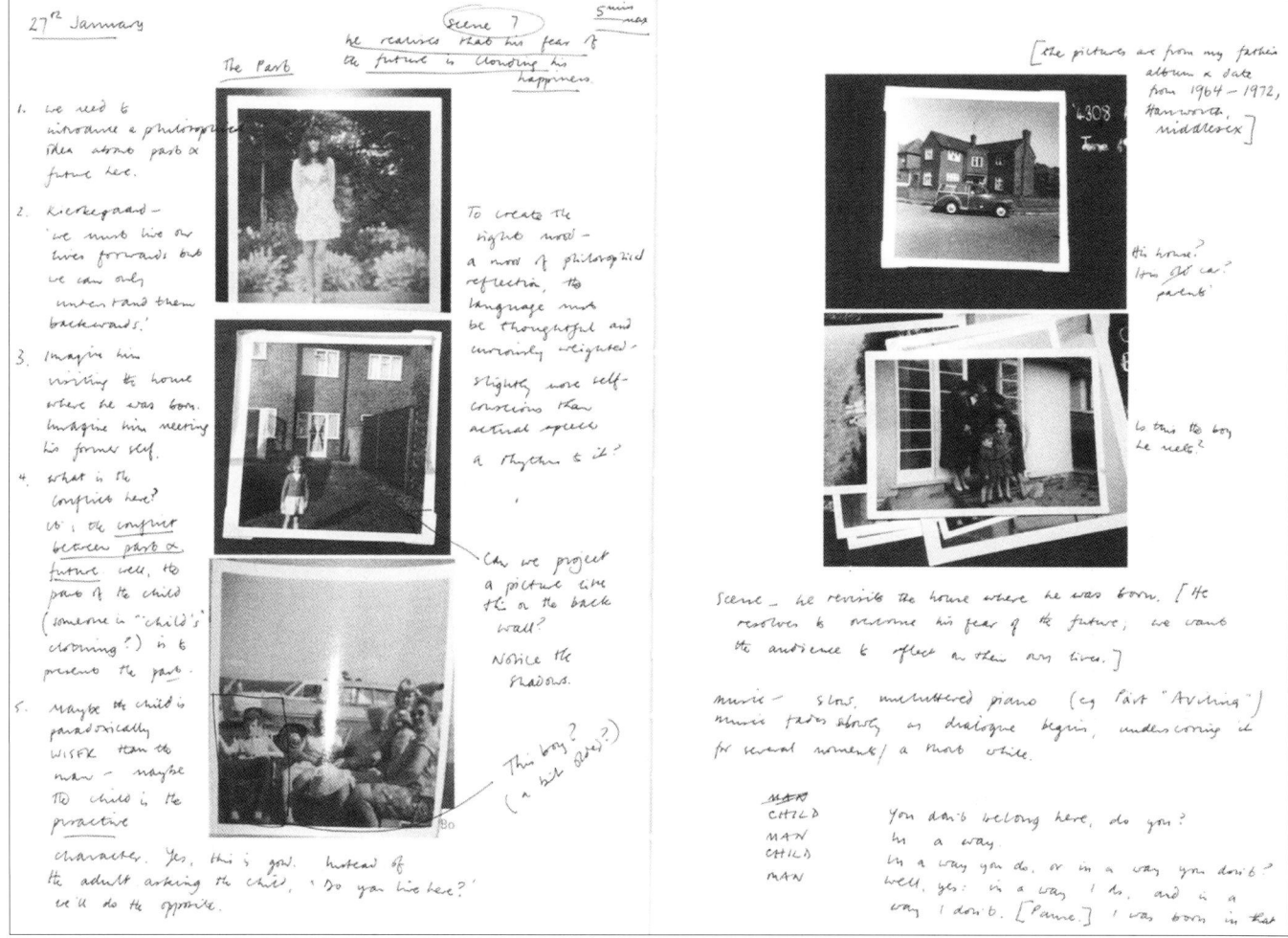

Health and safety

You need to show in your portfolio (and during your performance, of course) that you are aware of the health and safety issues involved in staging your piece. You need to be specific here, examining the precise health and safety implications thrown up by your piece, rather than being too general. Your teacher will help you identify what these are. However, the following are some general ideas to consider, to give you an idea of what sort of things you should be aware of, and to help you rehearse and perform safely and responsibly.

➤ Behave in a responsible manner when working in practical study situations.

➤ Wear clothing that is appropriate for practical drama work.

➤ All studios should have notices of fire exits and equipment.

➢ Naked flames must not be used in performance without prior consultation.

➢ Check carefully before standing on chairs or rostra to make sure they are on flat surfaces, are stable, and able to take your weight.

➢ When rehearsing fight sequences, make sure that you carefully rehearse the moves that make up the sequence in slow motion until you are sure mistakes will not be made. Always agree on a start signal so that no one is surprised.

➢ When engaging in any vigorous activity warm your body up with gentle exercise. Sudden or strong movement from cold can cause injury.

➢ Do not attempt heavy lifting; learn how to lift and bend properly.

➢ All set and scenery must be carefully secured with attention to balance and top-heavy construction.

➢ Cables should not cross any walkways unless they are fully taped and covered.

➢ Powered equipment, particularly lanterns, generate heat. Do not place such items in closed areas, nor near inflammable materials nor in a place where people can come into contact with them.

➢ In the case of stage lighting, rigging should be done without the power on.

A word of warning

As your portfolio nears conclusion, you need to look over it to make sure that it is a coherent whole. It may be a good idea, in the end, to use your 'scrapbook' as a basis for a well-organised, typed-up 2,000-word piece. You need to make sure that a new reader will make sense of your work and intentions. Of course, you should submit your scrapbook too, as a sort of appendix to your summary.

As we have said, there will be a diary element to your portfolio. The whole point of it is to trace the development of your ideas, after all. However, you must avoid a blandly descriptive diary which offers no interpretation. An entry such as 'Monday. We rehearsed the first scene. It went well. The lights did not work very well.' is not helpful!

Time management

Planning   At your first meeting, draw up a calendar that outlines the time your group will spend on each element of the preparation and rehearsal period, and show precisely when you will do the work. As a broad scenario, there are three sections to this work, and it is as well not to confuse them:

1.   First you must research and plan your piece, establishing aims and objectives and a basic shape and theme.

2.   Then you should complete a script with a detailed scenario that turns your ideas into something concrete.

3.   Finally, you should rehearse your script for performance.

Try not to mix these up. It is a bad sign if you're still not sure what your aims and objectives are when you have a script, and it is also a bad sign if you are still making whole-scale revisions to your script once you have entered the final rehearsal period. It's pretty disastrous, too, if your design team is not working closely in step with your acting team. Don't leave technical elements to the end.

You have to be honest with yourselves. You will not get everything done in the minimum time if you want to do it well. You need to build emergency sessions into your calendar. Don't just schedule them at the end of the process: setting yourselves clear deadlines for each stage of the process is really good practice.

You must all cooperate. If, when the calendar is being drawn up, it becomes obvious that one or more members of your group is hindering progress through a reluctance to commit themselves to dates and times, you must resolve this straight away. This is one of the very few occasions in your school or college life where the quality of your cooperation is assessed. Do not let your team down!

Suggested schedule

We recommend the following programme for preparing and developing your piece. A more detailed look at some of the individual stages can be found on later pages.

Planning, researching, shaping

1.   Considering a theme: research

Your theme must be related to other areas of your AS course. But what theme will you choose and how are you going to research this? Do not spend too long choosing a theme – at the end you'll need this time. Set yourself a time limit – when that time comes, make your decision and do not look back.

Too often, young actors and directors begin with the abstract and stay with it. Avoid this. By all means choose an abstract aim – aims are pretty philosophical anyway – but then immediately bring it down to earth, working out how you will convey it concretely.

Spend time researching your topic. Maybe this means spending hours in a shopping centre, taking photographs and jotting down fragments of conversation. Maybe it means arranging a tour of a local factory, or getting up absurdly early to see agriculture at work. Research, as we shall see, is very important.

2.   Improvisation and experimentation

Bring ideas back to the group. Explore some of them through improvisation and see what you find. This takes time, but you must be disciplined – do not spend too long just experimenting.

3.   A plan: shaping a scenario

At this stage, you should now be able to draft a scenario for your piece. What's going to happen? How will it be structured and shaped? Where are the climaxes? How does the pace quicken and slow? How should the audience react at each key moment? At this stage, you should be able to clarify precisely the objectives which have flowed from your aim. Having your scenario set down clearly is important and it is essential that each member of the group has a copy of this.

4. Discussing the whole

This is where you integrate acting ideas and design ideas: how will stage, set, style, costume, mask and language gel together (or strike against one another)? You might want to have a look at the work of Craig to give you some ideas here. There will be plenty to write in your portfolio as you set out the shape and the form of your piece.

Preparing a script

5. The script

Once you've set yourselves clear aims and objectives, and once you've designed a shape for your piece, you can get down to the nitty-gritty of devising scenes and speeches.

You can go back and adjust the shape of the piece after some work on scenes, obviously, but you should try and stick to your decisions and simply work through each problem as it occurs. Problems are best solved, rather than ignored or avoided.

Preparing a performance

6. Rehearsal

Rehearsal is not the same process as devising. You should now have a script. You will make some changes. There may be some cuts, maybe the odd re-write. But basically, the script you're holding is the script you're going to perform. You've moved to a new stage now: performing. Imagine how long a company would have working with a script. You have maybe three weeks! Do not pretend you're rehearsing when really you're re-writing and going over old ground pointlessly. Stick to your schedule!

7. Run-throughs and previews

Don't let the exam be the first time you've performed the piece for an audience. Perform it to another group of students – maybe the A2 group – so that you get a feel for the thing in performance and so you can get a response from an intelligent audience. You can also sort out technical gremlins.

An evening performance for parents and teachers is also an excellent plan. Set this date right at the start and keep to it.

The purpose of previews is to cast a critical eye over the piece. You may still want to make changes, maybe to the pace or to the lighting plot, or maybe to one or two speeches, where there may have been specific problems. Organising a preview is really valuable, but it's pretty pointless if you haven't built in time to evaluate it and make modifications. (This provides more material for the portfolio, of course.)

8. Time for last revisions and a dress rehearsal

The dress rehearsal is not a preview. It's a last opportunity to check everything works, and to check that everyone is ready to do their best.

Ignore the superstition which claims that when the dress rehearsal is poor, the show will be a hit: if the dress rehearsal is poor, you've got a problem. Do your very best. Then do it again for the exam.

Let's now break some of these key areas down and look at them in more detail.

Planning, researching and shaping

Research

Research is important: the ability to undertake good research and use the results relevantly is a key to getting good marks in this module. Research enables you to turn abstract ideas into concrete drama. Once you've settled on an idea that relates to your AS studies, draw up a list of research areas to share around the group. Then meet again after the research period – which needs to be short and concentrated – and review your tentative plans in the light of what you've seen and found out.

Good research will help you come up with interesting ideas. You might make a series of visits to gain information and insights. Such visits might also furnish you with the raw material for key speeches.

In his work with David Hare on *The Permanent Way*, a play that deals with the political, social and personal issues emerging from the decision to privatise British Rail, the director Max Stafford-Clark encouraged his cast to undertake considerable research. He described it himself like this:

> 'There was no script at this point, just a list of phone numbers and contacts with people who had been involved at different levels in the railway industry. We met bankers and civil servants involved in the original privatisation. We talked to several directors of major train operating companies. We talked to the bereaved and survivors of train crashes. Some of the actors spent time working as ticket collectors, clad in train uniforms; and others observed and talked to a track gang for several days. Everybody was happy to talk and keen to tell their story. At the start of each day, we would each report our encounters to the whole group. From these stories and these meetings David crafted this compelling play.

One research technique involved the actors interviewing key figures and then recreating the interview back at base for the rest of the cast. The actor would adopt the role and, as far as possible, voice and stance of the person interviewed and then give his testimony, answering questions and so on, improvising a character that had become fictional, but was based on scrupulous research.

Use your portfolio notebook to record your research, whether as a written account or as something more visual, such as photographs or diagrams. Good research is a test of your observational skills. Don't be afraid to stare! What's going on in those other motorway cars? What are those women actually talking about? Don't be afraid to speculate, either. Using your imagination to juxtapose and develop observed scenes is really a cornerstone in drama. Look closely at your raw material, and then ask yourself 'What happens next?' and try to come up with a convincing answer. It doesn't have to be observed scenes, either. Look through a set of local newspapers and cut out any interesting or relevant stories. Always ask yourself 'What happens next?'

Design factors

✦ Should set designers in your group undertake research by visiting actual places, or theatres or art galleries?

✦ Take care when researching using 'real' props. If your set requires a telephone box, making arrangements with BT to provide you with a dummy one is clever, but means that everything else in your set must have a similar degree of realism.

✦ The same argument applies to costume. It may not work dramatically for actors to wear realistic costumes. Exaggeration or stylisation may achieve more appropriate effects. You have to think about this (and note your debate and decisions in your portfolio).

Web link

For more on this, see the play's website at www.outofjoint.co.uk/prods/permanentway.html

Observation

Conflict

Some people will tell you that drama is founded on conflict: a conflict of personalities, of politics, of culture or values, of mood or atmosphere. Good research should give you the grounding for the form of your piece, for the language in which it will be voiced, and for the conflicts that will create the drama in it.

Art as inspiration

Maybe your idea doesn't lend itself to the kind of research where you can visit places and listen to real people. Maybe you have an idea you want to work with, but you can't find anything concrete to help you work on it. Sometimes, an afternoon spent leafing through books of paintings and photographs can throw up fascinating scenarios which will help solve this dilemma. Artaud, in *Theatre and its Double*, writes about how he was fascinated by the painting in the Louvre of *Lot and his Daughters*. He could see the drama implicit in the painting, and could in his imagination see a way of transforming the painting into a performance.

For more on Artaud, see pages 117–128.

Visit the website of the National Museums and Galleries of Wales. In their catalogue you will find an image of a painting called *Running away with the Hairdresser* by Kevin Sinnott, which is held in the National Gallery of Wales, Cardiff. Look at it closely. Think about it. Who are these characters (and which one is the hairdresser)? Where have they come from and where are they going? You can ask more questions along these lines and then move on to explore your starting point a little more elaborately. For example, what kind of mood is suggested by the painting? Is it a happy one or a sad one? A lonely one or an erotic one? How does the detail in the background contribute to the effect of the painting?

Web link

Go to www.nmgw.ac.uk/art/collections/db and search for Sinnott under Artist.

Finally, ask yourself the big questions. What does the painting mean? Is there any significance in the way the couple is running from the light into the shade? How do you read the gesture which is placed right in the centre of the painting? Is the gap between the hands growing or closing? What are the conflicts implicit here?

Design factors

Designers too can get plenty of ideas from works of art. David Hockney is just one of many modern painters who have made significant contributions to set design and mood setting.

Hazards

When you are preparing material in this way, here's a short list of dos and don'ts to consider. They are not set in stone, but you should think about them carefully.

Watch less television. This sounds absurd, but maybe it isn't so mad. Television drama has very different qualities from theatre. You might be amazed (and disappointed) to know just how many AS group productions try to ape television genres and forms. Chat shows, soaps, talent competitions and stand-up comedy are not the kind of things we're dealing with here, and it would be very difficult to imagine any AS group project which was able to pull off the incorporation of this kind of performance into the production. Anything which belongs on television should, quite simply, stay there.

You may want to consider the advantages and disadvantages of using video recordings of your rehearsals. Watching them back can be very helpful, especially for listening back to dialogue. Remember, though, that it's not a professionally filmed and edited recording and you're not on TV! Try not to be distracted by technical shortcomings and focus on what you're seeing as theatre.

Watch fewer films. Similarly, films use all sorts of techniques that do not transfer well to the theatre. Because the camera can cut away suddenly from a conversation, for example, short scenes can be very effective. In a theatre, where we have to concern ourselves with exits and entrances as well as with voice projection and stage presence, a short, intimate dialogue which cuts away to another scene can be cumbersome in performance and pretty unconvincing. Good theatre comes from the use of a language, as Artaud observed, which is uniquely theatrical. Film acting is a very different kind of skill.

See pages 117–128.

See more theatre. It's obvious, really, that if you are going to devise an effective piece of original drama you need to be as familiar as possible with drama in performance. Maybe you've seen some high-budget, large-scale productions of classic texts. How helpful are these? Although there is much we can learn from such productions, sometimes you can learn more from a small-scale production at a local arts centre where the equipment and space available are more comparable with what you probably have at your disposal at your school or college. Local universities and colleges can also be very useful. It's a good idea to have seen three or four such productions before you embark on this project.

What can you learn from such a production? Think about the structure of the piece; about the way it handles concrete imagery to suggest an abstract discussion; about how it moves from one scene to another; about the use of music, sounds, costume and lighting. What kind of acting techniques are required of a small-scale performance in a relatively intimate space? Are they the same as the skills required of a large-scale performance?

Sometimes you can learn a lot from a production that isn't entirely successful. What were your expectations before the performance? How could it have been better? Where exactly were the problems? What was the production trying to achieve, and where did it find difficulties?

Finally, **don't put the abstract first**: let it emerge. You may have started with a fairly abstract theme, such as 'to explore the effect of personal tragedy on a tightly-knit community', but when it comes to devising your production, you need to achieve this aim through *concrete* details: a real sense of community, a clear moment of tragedy, a thoughtful development and exploration of conflict and crisis. At your preview performances you should be able to evaluate whether your audience was able to distil the abstract idea – the meaning, if you like – from the concrete drama.

Developing a dramatic imagination

In order to achieve this concrete theatre from your abstract thoughts and from your research, you need to develop and practice using a more dramatic imagination.

It's easier to demonstrate this than explain it. Original drama does not have to be literal. Both research into the literal, actual world and metaphor are important, even if they lead in opposite directions to start with. The best realistic drama, such as Ibsen's and Strindberg's uses both metonymy and metaphor. Don't be afraid to use your imaginations. Base your drama on the actual, the possible, but don't be afraid to imagine the impossible.

See page 124 for more on metonymy and metaphor.

Rehearse the following scene. Try to notice the rhythms of the speech: the rhythms within each speech and, more importantly the rhythms created by the juxtaposition of the two voices. Think about set. Would a realistic set suit this dialogue? What would be the advantages and disadvantages of such a set? Hopefully this exercise will help you to think about dramatising the impossible, surreal or unlikely.

CHILD	You don't belong here, do you?
MAN	In a way.
CHILD	In a way you do, or in a way you don't?
MAN	Well, yes, in a way, I do, and in a way I don't. [Pause] I was born in that house.[Pause]
CHILD	My dad's?
MAN	Number 17.
CHILD	But you don't live there any more, do you?
MAN	Maybe not.
CHILD	[Pause] Are you grown up now? Are you a man?
MAN	I suppose I am. Though right now I'm imagining being a boy, here, in number 17.
CHILD	And are you happy? I'd like to be grown up.
MAN	I was happy, I think, but I don't know for sure. Maybe I was happy. Things were good. There were no problems; we didn't have any problems. Don't think so.
CHILD	What sort of problems?
MAN	I guess no one knows when they're really happy.
CHILD	What sort of problems? Do all adults have problems?
MAN	I think growing up is when you start to realise you have problems. [Pause] Money. Children. The future is full of problems.
CHILD	I don't care about the future. I don't know what the future is.
MAN	The future is the difference between you and me.
CHILD	The future is birthdays and the future is holidays. The future is a snow man on the rec and fireworks.
MAN	[Pause] Fireworks.
CHILD	What did you do when you lived here?
MAN	Well, I went to school.
CHILD	I go to school. I walk there every morning with my mother and then in the afternoon she collects me and we walk home.
MAN	I used to walk to school. The Oriel School. A mile through the estate.
CHILD	The Oriel.
MAN	If I had it all again. [Pause] If I had it all again, I wonder if it would all have been the same.
CHILD	It will all be the same. It will all be the same again.
MAN	Will it?
CHILD	I go to school. I walk there every morning with my mother and then in the afternoon she collects me and we walk home.
MAN	You don't belong here, do you?
CHILD	In a way.

MAN	In a way you do, or in a way you don't? [Pause]
CHILD	Well, yes, in a way, I do, and in a way I don't.
MAN	And what will happen next?
CHILD	You know what will happen next. You know.
MAN	I know.

Shaping and structuring

A play, even a short one, must have a strong structure to be successful. Although there is a lot of instinct in the way a playwright structures a play, there's a degree of cool analysis, too. As you are working in a group, you must try and articulate your own instincts and turn them into cool analysis.

Structure is important but its forms are very subtle. In Lorca's play *Yerma* there is very little change of mood: it's all very intense and highly-charged. This is deliberate, of course, and ensures that the final climax is a terrifying resolution. However, within the play there is a carefully controlled management of scenes. Some have just one or two characters in them, making them intense and intimate; others, like the scenes with the washerwomen or the ritual dance, have many characters on stage, which changes the feel of the piece without breaking its overall direction and intensity. Analysing the structure of a piece like this will reveal, as we shall see, the nuances of its construction.

> In this instance, Lorca seems to be following the model of Greek tragedy, where the alternation between 'character' sections and chorus sections has a similar effect.

Composers are deeply concerned with the structures of their music. Without a verbal language to pattern their pieces with articulated themes and ideas, they must rely on repetition and development to create the emotional and intellectual effects they seek. Pay attention to the structure of some familiar (or even some unfamiliar) pieces of music. Notice how repetition is used to develop ideas; notice the use of a theme and its variations. Notice where the climaxes occur and the function of the introduction and the coda. Romantic music tends to finish like a Shakespearean play: there's a huge flourish, and we are in no doubt about the fact that the piece has concluded. Modern music, like modern drama, is a little more ambiguous: the endings seem more open.

Music

> This sense of structure is not limited to what one might call classical music. Bands like Radiohead and Sigur Ros also structure their pieces very carefully using key changes and repetition to pattern their music.

Further study

Find out about sonata form in music. Can a play be written in this form? What would be the benefits?

Photos

You might find it useful when shaping your piece to take digital photographs of moments in your piece. By pinpointing such key moments, you are shaping the piece; by photographing them, you are clarifying ideas about design and staging; by using the photographs to structure your piece, you are thinking carefully about the placing of climaxes, and the overall movement of the piece. If you are the group's designer, you may find digital photographs very useful – using a computer program such as Adobe Photoshop will enable you to manipulate images to experiment with different design elements – the use of coloured lighting, for example.

Clocks

In 1967, Paul McCartney and John Lennon sketched out their ideas for the Beatles' film *The Magical Mystery Tour* as a kind of wheel or clock. They divided the planned film into slices and then filled each one. Their idea was to create a balanced structure by seeing the whole as a series of complementary parts.

> "Paul and John sat down in Paul's place in St John's Wood. They drew a circle, and then marked it off like the spokes on a wheel. It was a case of "We can have a song here, and a dream sequence there," and so on. They mapped it out."
>
> Neil Aspinall, in *The Beatles Anthology* (Cassell 2000).

Let's borrow this idea. If you study a play carefully, you will see that it is structured through a series of episodes (which may or may not be quite the same as 'scenes'). Some episodes will be fast in pace, light or humorous in tone and full of characters; others may be slow in pace, heavy, tragic or thoughtful in tone and may employ just one or two voices. You will also find that repetition is used as part of structure. In *Hamlet* there are comic and (relatively) light scenes, but the play is structured around slow, thoughtful scenes in which Hamlet is either alone or with just one or two other characters. By examining the structure of the play, we have discovered something (rather obvious, maybe) about its meaning and how this meaning is achieved. Comedies can be broken down in the same way: they tend to incorporate scenes which have a faster pace and which use a greater number of parts. But there may still be key episodes (as there are in *Twelfth Night*) where things take a more tragic turn with slow, thoughtful scenes involving just two or three characters.

When we plan our time-wheel, we should think about all this. It's actually a good idea to start by analysing a play you're already studying through a clock structure. You'll see then how the system works, and how your play works, too. You might be surprised by the insights provided by analysing the structure of a play in this way. Scenes whose function seemed cloudy or vague suddenly make sense: they are needed to break up the monotony of one theme or to balance a similar scene elsewhere. For an example of such a time-wheel, see the inside back cover of this guide.

When you've done that, you'll be ready to work on your own scheme. You might start by deciding, for example, that as your piece is going to be a thoughtful and solemn piece about a serious issue, most of your slices will be slow-paced, thoughtful and relatively solitary affairs. You might particularly want the first and last scenes to be of this serious nature. You might balance this with busier scenes and some humour. You will place the climaxes at appropriate points, which may be a little way before the end, so that there can be a final, reflective scene. And so on.

You'll probably need to annotate your time-wheel with arrows and colours to show the use of motifs and other structural material.

Sound

You may consider using sound to shape the mood of your piece. Now that you've made a start with your time-wheel, maybe you could use a computer to create a collage of different kinds of music, each capturing the mood of each slice of your clock pie, with repetitions to echo repetitions in your chosen structure. If you play this during some early run-throughs, you'll be able to use sound to help establish and maintain mood and to control pace. This can be very effective.

Design factors

Designers may want to attach colours to each slice or comment about the intensity of light, so that they can consider developments and changes in mood and atmosphere.

Preparing a script

Subtext

For more on subtext, see the explanation on page 25 of the Understanding Theatre section.

When you are devising your script, remember the importance of subtext. Your piece will be short in theatrical terms, so don't waste a line. It's no good just showing us breakfast. We have all seen people pass the sugar: it's not interesting. What we want to see is a breakfast where, for example, lovers are suddenly revealed to each other in the unforgiving morning light, no longer the young things of the evening before. We want to hear the anxiety and doubt in their voices, anxieties and doubts about their relationship and about the adult jealousies which are beginning to form in their minds. When a character like this asks for the sugar, we read all sorts of things into the gesture that is offered in reply, the lack of eye contact, the silence. In the subtext we hear the real relationship developing. Breakfast suddenly becomes interesting.

There are good examples in the chapter on Stanislavski about subtext and practical work related to it. For now, let us build on this and use an extract from Chekhov's *Uncle Vanya* to demonstrate the work that actors and director can do to explore emotion through action.

Uncle Vanya

Enter ASTROV with a map.

ASTROV Good afternoon.

He shakes hands with her.

You wanted to see what I've been painting?

YELENA You promised yesterday you'd show me your work. Can you spare the time?

ASTROV Of course.

He spreads the map out on the card-table and fixes it with drawing pins.

Where were you born?

YELENA *(Helps him)* St Petersburg.

ASTROV And where did you study?

YELENA At the conservatoire.

ASTROV You may not find this very interesting.

YELENA Why not? I don't know the country, it's true, but I've read a lot.

ASTROV I've got my own work-table in the house here. In Vanya's room. When I get completely exhausted, and I can't think properly any more, I drop everything and come running over here to distract myself with this thing for an hour or two. Vanya and Sonya click away on the abacus, and I sit beside them at my table, busy with my colouring, and it's warm and peaceful, and the cricket chirps. I don't allow myself this pleasure very often, though – once a month *(Indicates the map)*.

Now, look at this. It represents this part of the country as it was fifty years ago. The light and dark green colouring indicates forest; half of the entire surface-area is forest. Where the green is hatched with red there were elk and wild goats. I've indicated the fauna as well as the flora. On this lake there were swans and geese and ducks, and what the old people call a power of birds of every sort – the place was swarming with them. Apart from the villages, look, you can see a scattering of various settlements and smallholdings, little monasteries, watermills. Cattle and horses were abundant. They're marked in blue. This district, for example, was thick with blue; there were complete herds, and two or three horses per farm.

(Pause) Now let's look down here. As it was twenty-five years ago. By this time only a third of the surface-area is under forest. The goats have gone, but there are still elk. The green and blue are paler now. And so on, and so on. Let us move on to the third section – the district as it is today. There's green here and there, but it's not solid, it's only in patches; the elk, the swans, and the capercaillies have all

vanished. Of the former settlements, smallholdings, monasteries, and mills – not a trace. Overall it's the picture of a gradual but incontrovertible decline, which by the look of it will be complete in another ten or fifteen years. You'll tell me that civilizing factors are at work here, that the old life must naturally give way to the new. And, yes, I see that if these ruined forests had been replaced by roads and railways, if there were factories and schools here, then the peasants would be healthier and wealthier and wiser – but nothing of the kind!

The district still has the same swamps and mosquitoes, the same lack of roads, the same poverty and typhus and diphtheria and fires. What we are faced with here is a decline resulting from the unequal struggle for existence, a decline brought about by stagnation, by ignorance, by a total lack of awareness, by frozen, sick, and hungry men who, to preserve the last flickers of life, to save their children, instinctively, blindly, grasp at anything they can use to relieve their hunger and warm themselves, and who destroy it all without thought for the morrow. Almost everything has been destroyed now; and nothing yet has been created in its place.

(Coldly) I see from your face that you're not interested.

YELENA   I understand so little about it.

ASTROV   There's nothing to understand – you're simply not interested.

YELENA   I was thinking about something else, to tell you the truth. Forgive me.

 Consider the following subtexts:

1. Astrov and Yelena are madly in love with one another but have never been able to say so.

2. Yelena loves Astrov madly but he seems oblivious to her charms.

3. Astrov finds Yelena boring but wants to use her as an intermediary in order to meet Sonya, her step daughter, with whom he is infatuated.

4. Yelena finds Astrov boring but wants to introduce him to Sonya who is infatuated with him.

5. Yelena lusts after Astrov but he is gay.

6. Everyone has told Astrov that Yelena loves him – except Yelena herself!

7. Yelena's husband is having an affair with Astrov's wife.

8. Astrov and Yelena were engaged to be married but are now happily married to others.

9. Yelena wants to ask Astrov to lend her some money but she's bored stiff by his maps!

How does each of these statements affect the way the piece is performed? How are the actions different? Work in pairs on one each of these scenarios, and present yours to the group. Which is most convincing? Why?

Once you've read the scene through, you'll get the gist. Act it out without a script – that's important – improvising as accurately as you can the opening and final exchanges, and the long speech about the land-use maps. Which is the 'true' situation, do you think? Notice how by adding a subtext to our performance we are

Reproduced with permission, taken from *Uncle Vanya* by Anton Chekhov, translated by Michael Frayn (Methuen 1987).

If you've read *Uncle Vanya*, you'll know that some of the versions given above simply cannot be true. But an audience seeing the play for the first time may be weighing up several such possibilities.

turning a lecture about Russian land-use into something a lot more interesting.

Shaping ideas as a group

You've got to work together to develop your piece: as we have noted before, cooperation and dividing up labour are key to success. You must fight lead-actor syndrome – everyone must contribute on an equal footing – but also you must fight modesty.

One technique for moving from ideas to a script involves working in threes or fours on improvising dialogue. Once you have established the basic shape and function of a scene, you can begin improvising it, using your own words. Maybe two or three actors are required to play characters in the scene. A third or fourth member of the group (perhaps the designer, if you have one) simply listens, but notes down any moment, interchange, reaction or line that is really effective. After you've gone through the scene, the note-taker will report to the group and, after some discussion, you can agree to keep in some of these effective pieces. Work through the piece again, maybe this time taking different roles. The point is to allow the piece to emerge from disciplined improvisation: achieving this is key to making progress.

Improvisation

It may be useful here to borrow some ideas from language study. In analysing spoken language in dialogue and conversation, three forms of behaviour can be identified. Sometimes, one of the characters will be proactive, leading discussion and prompting developments and decisions; other characters will be reactive, following the lead set by the more pro-active members. (You may well find your own group begins like this, before you move on to a more equitable arrangement!) Ideally, your group will represent a third stance: collaboration.

In improvising scenes, it can be useful to identify proactive, reactive and collaborative characters. You will find that such discussions will also shed light on the relative status of the characters.

You won't all be choosing acting as your specific skill. This doesn't mean, of course, that you shouldn't all take part in preliminary improvisation sessions. In many ways, involving all the group in such sessions can be a very good strategy. However, if you are focusing on a design skill, you must make sure that as the work progresses, your design ideas are strong and individual.

Designers

Evaluating ideas

After you have spent some time preparing scenes and dialogues, you need to evaluate them. The process of devising and now the process of evaluation will give you plenty to write about in your portfolio.

You need to ask yourselves questions about how you want the audience to react, what you want them to think about and how you want them to feel. This is the point where design ideas about costume, use of mask (if any), set, sound and lighting need to be fully integrated and discussed, whether you are focusing on this element rather than acting, or whether the design features are

Design

going to be shared around the group. Some key ideas will need to be discussed alongside the devising of the first scenes. You don't need to make firm decisions straight away – you should spend some time during each of the early sessions reviewing staging decisions: where is the piece going to be performed, on what kind of stage/set, with what costumes and sound effects?

Rationale

Do not make hasty decisions. You must have a rationale for your decisions. If you decide, as Artaud might have done, to hold your play in a barn or a hangar (this seems unlikely, but the point is clear), you must have a reason, and the reason must relate to your initial aims and objectives, too. All of this should be noted in your portfolio. Even if you do not have a designated designer, do not leave decisions about set, lighting and props until the end. Make the look and sound of the play organic. (As we have suggested, look at the work of Craig to see how important this was to him.) Always keep your primary aim in mind.

Producing a script

At some point, even if you are working from a detailed scenario, you will have to write something down. Ideally, you will produce a script that you will work with professionally during your preparation and rehearsal sessions.

There are some key points to add here. Keep in mind that this is still an ensemble piece: make sure you work together, even if you have a talented writer in your group who takes the lead in some areas. Evaluation and analysis are important roles for everyone.

Language

Writing a play is not easy. You must understand the artificiality of theatrical language. Although you may have jotted down some phrases you've heard spoken, either during research or during improvisation sessions, a script that relies exactly on the language people use as they go about their daily business will be a very dull script. And although interruptions and unfinished utterances are natural in life, these don't always work on stage, and must be used with care.

Have a look again at the extract from Chekhov's *Uncle Vanya* and at the scene between the MAN and CHILD. Note how both take the ordinary language of daily life and heighten it for the stage. Try to imagine how this conversation might actually sound in reality: more fragmentary, perhaps, with fewer grammatically correct sentences; different kinds of pauses; slang or more phatic language and so on. It can be a good idea to spend some time reading a play script – maybe just re-reading a text you're studying – to remind yourselves of the special kind of artificial language which all plays use. You need to think explicitly about the tone your characters achieve, and about the tone of the play. The precise choice of language will influence pace and feel, and you may need to rework the wording to get the effect just right. This will take time and care.

Phatic refers to the type of speech that expresses our sociability rather than communicating ideas or information. So for instance, to say 'Good morning, how are you today?' or perhaps to discuss the weather is to use phatic language.

It is a huge mistake to think you can improvise during your final performance. In this module, improvisation is a tool, not a product. Improvisation will lean quite heavily towards the norms of your own expression. This is fine: but in a performance your character must have his or her own idiolect. Working on this, as playwrights

Someone's idiolect is their own characteristic way of speaking, their personal language.

from Shakespeare to Congreve and Chekhov have done, is an important part of playwriting. Scripts produced through improvisation require some editing to bring out the different flavours of the characters' voices and use of language.

Remember the old saying: 'everything is bigger on stage'. This is true of language, too. The language of all your characters will be a kind of heightened version of the real language we'd expect to meet in daily life. Look again at your set texts and see just how true this is.

Preparing a performance

Actioning the text

When Stanislavski worked on Chekhov's plays, notably *Three Sisters* and *The Cherry Orchard*, he constantly wrote to Chekhov, then living in the Crimea, to ask for advice and explanation regarding the text. Obviously this is not always possible. In his book *Letters to George* (Nick Hern Books 1997), director Max Stafford-Clark explains how he too is used to dealing with contemporary playwrights in this manner. But he goes on to detail the rehearsals for a production of a restoration play by George Farquhar, who had been dead for over 200 years and therefore was not able to reply to letters nor answer the phone. Stafford-Clark's solution to this was to write down a report of each day's work as a letter to the playwright, sharing anxieties, articulating problems, and praising effective and successful scenes.

Letters to George

In other words, the book is a giant example of a working portfolio. At this stage of the preparation process, you too could write letters or diary entries reporting on progress. Of course, as one of the devisers of the piece, you should be able to answer some of the problems or question how things have developed. All of this is very valuable.

In *Letters to George*, Stafford-Clark outlines a brilliant rehearsal technique based on actioning the text. Firstly, he starts his rehearsals with a script, with the actors sitting around a table (remember that he's already asked them to undertake key research activities to inform their understanding of the play and of their roles within it). The focus is on the text and breaking it down to understand what is behind what the characters say. That's one reason why it is so important, after all your experimentation, improvisation, writing and editing, to produce a polished, written script.

Actioning

The idea behind Stafford-Clark's actioning technique is this: when people speak, especially in a play, it is not idle chatter, or saying words merely for the sake of saying them. There is some motivation behind their words. For instance, they may be threatening someone, warning someone, or flirting with someone – they are performing some action through speaking. Stafford-Clark argues that a key role of rehearsal is to establish just what action each speech – or each section of a longer speech – is fulfilling. He and his cast would take each speech, or section of speech, and decide what the speech is *doing*, what its purpose in the play is. After discussing

Examples of transitive verbs can be found in italics in the following sentence: 'The mother *detains* her son. He *ignores* her.' A transitive verb always has an object: you cannot say 'The mother detains', you have to say who or what she detains, because the action is not one she can do on her own.

See page 107.

See *Blood Wedding*, translated by Michael Dewell and Carmen Zapata in *The House of Bernarda Alba and Other Plays* by Federico García Lorca (Penguin 2001).

this, they would agree on a transitive verb that they think explains what this action is, for example, to threaten, to warn, or to detain. By discussing each speech in this way with the group, you will soon find how collaborative a process this is. You will also find that it should become much easier to act the play out afterwards. You focus on the underlying and agreed action of the speech as you deliver it. This will affect, for example, the pace and tone of your voice, your gestures and your body language. Since the action is represented by a transitive verb and therefore shows the effect of the speech on others, it will also influence where you put yourself on stage and how you react to the other characters. In Stanislavski's terms, it will affect the size of your circle of attention. It will also affect your relationship with the audience; after all, in some Restoration dramas, the action of a lot of the speeches is to inform the audience.

Devising actions to accompany text requires an understanding of what is really going on. In *Blood Wedding* by Lorca, the Mother's opening lines, are, on the face of it, pretty meaningless; what she really wants is simply to hold her son in conversation to delay his departure because she is protective of him. On the other hand, he hesitates because he wants to bring up the question of his marriage. There is more to this than a simple departure for work. Consider the following interpretation.

Text	Comments	Suggested action verbs
BRIDEGROOM *[entering]* Mother?	Why does a grown man tell his mother that he is leaving for work? Why does he need to attract her attention? Does he really want to talk about his plans for marriage? There are many interpretations. The beauty of the 'actioning' technique is that the cast clarifies its view and maintains a consistent interpretation of events. Maybe the bridegroom does want to talk about his marriage, as becomes a little clearer later in the scene, so is testing the water with this word. Very tentative.	The bridegroom **tests** his mother.
MOTHER Yes.	One word. But look more closely. Is the mother asking her son what he wants? Is she exasperated with him? Does she know what's coming – the question of marriage? Is she resisting this? (You'll notice how important it is for this kind of analysis that the cast knows the entire script and has a feel for the overall aims and objectives of the text.)	The mother **resists** her son. Try this in performance. Say the one word, 'Yes', in a way which resists the person who has just addressed you.

Script	Commentary	Action
BRIDEGROOM I'm going.	It sounds as if he's chickened out. We can all see he's going. Has he paused before his answer? Does this indeed confirm our feelings that in the first instance he was testing his mother out to see what sort of mood she was in, and whether now was a good time to talk about his fiancée? In which case this is a bit of a climb-down.	The bridegroom **subordinates** himself to his mother.
MOTHER Where?	She knows. He works on the land; he's just bought a vineyard. Obviously that's where he's going (you would know this, having thoroughly read and researched the text before the exercise). So she's not asking a question. She's challenging him, to come out with his wedding news perhaps.	The mother **challenges** the bridegroom.
BRIDEGROOM To the vineyard. *[He starts to go.]*	Complete surrender. He's off, without having talked about his life.	The bridegroom **surrenders** to his mother.
MOTHER Wait.	Why? They're definitely skirting this issue, aren't they? Perhaps the mother is delaying her son to protect him (from the future) or so that they can talk about the wedding (which is what happens).	The mother **invites** her son (to continue).
BRIDEGROOM Do you need something?	This could be aggressive or kind, on the face of it. But maybe he is frustrated with the way the mother is playing with his emotions. He could sound quite exasperated? Maybe he now is taking the upper hand, challenging his mother to talk about the future? Maybe he is challenging her; maybe he is rejecting her.	The bridegroom **challenges** his mother.

There are many ways of rehearsing a script, but finding 'actions' to accompany the text can be an important start to the process of converting script to performance. You will need a good vocabulary, so having a thesaurus to hand is a good idea. You might just glue your script into your portfolio, and work on it there, producing a table like this, so that your portfolio directly records the discussions of the group and the final decisions.

Rehearsal techniques

Once you've begun rehearsals, you are no longer devising – you are rehearsing. You may find you need to make slight changes to the script to match other performance issues, but these should be few and minor. If you get to the designated rehearsal period and you're still devising, you've got a problem! Sometimes, it can be best to pretend at this stage that you are actually preparing a production of

Rehearsing not devising

someone else's play. That way, you focus on production issues and rehearsal techniques, and leave behind for good the questions of devising and structuring.

Design   You are working as a team. Design ideas must be integrated with rehearsals. If you are focusing on a design element for this module you must not work in isolation; nor should you go off and bring back your work two days before the dress rehearsal. As a team you should set out a carefully considered calendar of deadlines, so that lighting plots, soundscapes, costume, set, props and so on are prepared as they are needed, and are tested in rehearsal conditions.

Directing   To gain a high grade in this module, you need to respond positively to feedback and be objective in your assessment of how far your piece meets your original aims. Your play will need to be directed, and although your teacher will be able to give you feedback and some advice while your work is in progress, they will certainly not direct the play for you! But, at the same time, you must work as a team. Take it in turns to stand back from performing to look at the effect and to concentrate on individual scenes as they are being rehearsed. Don't look in the first place for solutions: try to identify problems. If something doesn't feel right, then it probably isn't right. The director should identify moments when something doesn't feel right, but it's best if the team discusses the issue and comes up with one or more solutions to try out. This in turn provides more grist for your portfolio.

When you're acting as a director, resist the temptation to interrupt a scene. This can ruin the concentration of the performers, and can disrupt the rehearsal so much that you never actually get to the end of the scene. The best practice is to give notes: jot down good things and problems as the scene is rehearsed, and then go through these notes quickly at the end, for whole-group discussion. Take this role in turns. It's your job as a team to respond to the comments. Don't be frightened of adverse remarks: they are really what you need. If there are problems, you need to be aware of them, so they can be solved.

It is very important to aim to perform your final, examined, piece without prompts at any time. But problems can arise, so make sure you have strategies in place to keep going. Identify any tricky areas and make sure you know how you can help one another on stage.

And finally, don't neglect the benefits of studying a practitioner. The work you have done on Stanislavski, Artaud or Craig should obviously help you with a range of rehearsal skills and ideas. Don't partition your course so that your three modules are separate, discrete areas that do not inform one another. Your practical performance should, in some key ways, represent a synopsis of all you have learned in your AS course.

Performance preparation

As the day of the examined performance approaches, you will feel increasingly anxious. This is a good thing. But you must adopt the kind of behaviour which will not exacerbate the tension.

Keep your space tidy. It's amazing how frustrating it is to rehearse in a space where the cast has abandoned its bags and coats all over the place as they have arrived. It's maddening when props are moved or carelessly discarded. Keep unnecessary stuff out of the theatre, and be orderly and cooperative about the props you require.

Punctuality is essential during the whole module, naturally, but now it is paramount. Everyone will be on edge, so a five-minute delay when one member of the cast turns up late for a rehearsal can produce huge anxiety and ruin the value of the session. You may be sharing a space with another group: this is another reason for tidiness and punctilious time-keeping. Turn up well organised and in good time.

Be organised

You will be very stressed, so make an effort to adopt quite formal manners. It's amazing how a little casual comment can provoke friction at this stage! By adopting careful spoken manners and by thinking first before speaking, a lot of stress can be dissipated. This may sound old-fashioned, but it's excellent advice. Being polite can help you to avoid communicating your own anxieties.

Relationships

You are working together. Everyone knows about the acting profession's 'luvvie' culture – don't be ashamed of this. When you're feeling anxious or nervous, it can be really helpful if a friend and colleague tells you how well you're doing. Go out of your way to praise your partners. Help one another to feel good about what you are doing and you will all do it better.

Try to create an ambience in your performance space so that you find it easy to establish the mood of your piece. Consider background music as you (and later, the audience) arrive; think about the exact quality of the 'house lighting' as you undertake those final rehearsals. You may not want a battery of strip lights, even when you are not using your final lighting plot. Ambience in these final sessions can be very helpful.

Atmosphere

Put aside time for completing your portfolio. Don't mix rehearsal time with portfolio time. Your portfolio is now almost entirely a personal and independent thing: work on it independently. Don't irritate others by claiming rehearsal time for yourself!

The portfolio

Finally, when it comes to the performance itself, the key thing is concentration. Remembering all that you have worked for and trying to help one another are essential elements of a successful performance. So are appropriate levels of performance energy and a tight focus. Prepare for all this by having a good night's sleep, arriving in plenty of time and drinking plenty of water. You should then be able to give your best – do not rely on luck.

Approaches to Text

Getting started

In this chapter we shall look at ways of exploring the set texts from a performance perspective. The starting point for any performance taken from a script is of course the text itself, but the end point – the production – is a combination of the input of everyone who works on that production from the director through to the props-maker. Therefore we can watch many productions of *A Midsummer Night's Dream*, for example, and all will be different. For the purpose of this examination you will need to look specifically at the input of the actor, the director and the designer. The questions you will be asked in the examination require you to answer from the standpoint of **one** of these three perspectives. Therefore, later in the chapter we will look at each of these contributors in turn, examining the ways they approach a text and come to decisions about how they wish to see that text in performance, with reference to the eight plays set for AS study.

Audience response

One of the most important questions you will need to answer while working out how you would produce a text is: What audience response do you wish to achieve? What reaction do you want your audience to leave the auditorium with? If you are acting the title role in *Antigone* for instance, do you want them to feel sympathy for Antigone, or to feel that she should have abided by the laws of state to preserve society? If you are directing *The Shadow of a Gunman,* is it more important that your audience are amused and moved by the emotions in the play, or that they learn about the politics of life in the tenements of Dublin in 1920? If you are designing a production of *Yerma*, will you give your audience a naturalistic impression of Andalusia in the 1930s that makes them appreciate the stifling, claustrophobic atmosphere, or will you give them a more poetic, expressionistic view of Lorca's world, which will allow them to reflect on the themes of desire and sterility of life in the play?

Interpreting the text

In order to answer these questions it is necessary for you to decide upon your interpretation of the text. You might think that any interpretation is valid and in many ways that is true, but only if you can justify that interpretation from the text; the text must support your idea. Thus one of the main skills being looked for here – and one we will be focusing on in this chapter – is the ability to justify your ideas. It is no good as a designer setting a production of *Three Sisters* in a small flat in the middle of 1960s London just because you think it will 'look good' or because you have access to some wonderful 1960s clothing; the fact that there is little in the text to support this setting means you will have to re-think this idea. Always start from the text, not random ideas.

You will of course have your copy of the play with you in the examination hall. You are allowed simple annotations in the form of highlighting, underlining or brief margin notes of two or three words, but not extensive comments. However, by the time you have finished working on the text, you will have little need of it in the exam other than for accurate quotations and quick reminders, and if you use it for more than this you will leave yourself no time to answer the exam question.

First reading

Before looking specifically at the role of the director, designer and actor, there are some important general guidelines that are useful to follow when starting work on a text. When reading through the play for the first time (and this should really be done quite quickly) keep notes of your first impressions such as anything that strikes you about the text or any visual idea you may have about staging. It is not necessary to understand every word of a text on first reading, but you are likely to pick up some of the overall themes and ideas within the play, so make a note of these.

Consider:

➢ What is the genre of the play?

➢ Which characters do you instinctively feel sympathy for?

➢ Which sections of the play have a fast pace and which seem slow?

➢ Does the play have a recognisable subplot and how does it seem to relate to the main plot?

➢ What problems immediately strike you in terms of staging the play? Solving those problems will become the most important element of working on a production; and as you work through this chapter you will find that this is what we keep coming back to.

It is also important to hear the words. There is a vast difference in reading a play in your head and in speaking the words out loud. The sound they make and the feel of them in your mouth adds a whole new element that must be taken into account. This is especially true of period plays, where the use of language is so different from our own 21st-century language. In fact, all eight plays on the set-text list have a distinctive sound to their language.

Having read the play through and heard some of the text spoken aloud, you should now have a collection of notes and unanswered questions, which will form the starting point of your work on the production of your set text. The next stage is to do some background work on the text.

Research

With any text it is vital to do research to establish the play's social and cultural context, knowledge of which is one of the requirements of this examination. Without research the production is likely to lack resonance for its audience and you may well do a great disservice to the play. The first research you do should be into the playwright, their background and life circumstances, and to find out if possible why they wrote the play. If there are any details

In the exam

You may find it helpful to have two copies of the text. One of these you can use throughout the year and write all over as you work on the play. The second you can keep to annotate clearly and precisely for the exam. The process of transferring your key points on to the second copy will be useful revision.

available on the first staging of the play these can be helpful in assessing the playwright's intentions. It is also important to set the play in its place in theatre history. It may be that the playwright was writing a typical piece of theatre for their time, or that they were trying to change the nature of theatre and to explore new ideas in theatrical form. If you have no comprehension of the original intention of the playwright then you are unlikely to have a real understanding of how the play will work in production and what you should be saying to your audience.

Set texts

Ideas concerning how to interpret and produce a set text according to the performance perspective will form the bulk of this chapter. But as we have seen, it is vital to understand the context of the play, and the following background information should provide you with a starting point, as well as suggestions for further study.

Antigone

Sophocles was born near Athens in 495 BCE, the son of a wealthy merchant. He studied the arts and at the age of 16 was chosen to lead a choir of boys to celebrate the victory at Salamis. He first competed in the City Dionysia (the annual festival to celebrate Dionysus, during which new plays were presented) some 12 years later and took first prize. He went on to write more than 100 plays and won 18 first prizes. Sophocles acted in his own plays on occasions and was considered to be a good actor, though his voice was rather weak. He also served as an ordained priest: this combination of actor and priest was common at this time, due to the religious nature of the festivals.

Sophocles changed the nature of theatre in two important ways. He added the third actor and also made each play entire in itself instead of writing in trilogies, as had been the custom. Each play was therefore more dramatically compact and events and thoughts occur much more quickly than in the earlier trilogy plays. Of his plays only seven complete scripts remain, of which *Oedipus* and *Antigone* are generally considered to be his greatest. Although *Antigone* is in some ways a sequel to *Oedipus*, it was in fact written first. The character of Creon is notably quite different in the two plays and this can present problems for the modern actor when the plays are performed together with *Oedipus at Colonus* (the middle play in plot sequence) as has been the recent custom.

Antigone, written and performed around 441 BCE, examines the conflict between loyalty to personal beliefs and political loyalty, as Antigone defies the orders of the king to do what she feels is her family obligation. Antigone's two brothers, Polyneices and Eteocles have recently fought and killed one another over the rule of Thebes. Since Eteocles was the legitimate heir and Polyneices had returned from exile in an attempt to gain the throne from him, Creon, the king of Thebes, decrees that Polyneices' body must be left to rot without burial. Antigone refuses to let the body of her brother go unburied, declaring Creon's order to go against divine law, and she disobeys the king, despite protests from her sister

Further reading

There are many general texts that can help you do this. Try *The Seven Ages of Theatre* by Richard Southern (Faber and Faber 1968); *The Theatre: a concise history* by Phyllis Hartnoll (Thames and Hudson 1998); *British Drama* by Allardyce Nicoll (Harrap 1978).

Sophocles

To understand *Antigone* fully, you will need a general grasp of Greek theatre and its concepts: for this, see pages 19–20.

Further study

Look at the way Greek theatre was presented: the natural structure of the theatres and how this aided projection; the use of masks and costumes to represent character; the formal use of verse and language. Find out what you can about Aristotle's Unities of Time, Place and Action; the meaning of catharsis; *Oedipus* and *Oedipus at Colonnus*.

The play

It was believed that burial – even just a token covering – was necessary in order for the spirit of the dead person to pass to the underworld. It was customary to bury even bitter enemies in order to prevent the pollution of the rotting corpse offending the gods.

Ismene. Creon is furious at Antigone's actions and, even though she is engaged to his own son Haemon, declares that she must be buried alive for defying him. After initially rejecting the advice of the seer Teiresias, Creon does finally relent in fear. It proves to be too late, however. Antigone has already hanged herself and Haemon, trapped between his future wife and his father, attacks Creon, but kills himself. After hearing the news, Eurydice, wife of Creon and mother of Haemon, also commits suicide. Creon is left, destroyed by the loss of his family.

A Midsummer Night's Dream

Although now one of Shakespeare's most popular and most produced plays, *A Midsummer Night's Dream* has not always been so valued. Samuel Pepys wrote in his diary in 1662, 'It is the most insipid, ridiculous play I ever saw in my life', and there are very few documents relating to its early performances, suggesting it was not often performed in Shakespeare's time. It has been suggested that the play was written in the mid 1590s to grace the wedding of a nobleman, and that the parts of Theseus and Hippolyta would have been played by the married couple at its first performance – Theseus is certainly portrayed as a romantic hero of the medieval age, despite his classical name. However, there is no clear proof of this. It is very different from any other play by Shakespeare, due to its inclusion of tiny fairies and a dream world. The play also mocks the more amateur theatrical groups of the time with the play-within-the-play of Pyramus and Thisbe, which suggests a personal amusement behind its writing. The play would also have required an unusually large number of boy actors to perform, which may have been another reason for fewer performances.

The play examines in a highly comic way the precariousness of human relationships. The end of the play brings four sets of lovers together after some considerable confusion and break-ups along the way. Although we are left with some doubt as to the successful continuation of all of these relationships, we are amused enough and entertained enough to accept them. By sending his human lovers into the magical world of the fairies, Shakespeare is able to speed up the process and problems of courtship through the device of a magic potion. Alongside this, the play uses the Mechanicals (artisans or workmen) to have fun with the notion of acting and a player's relationship with his audience, even to the extent of Puck asking for applause at the end 'if we be friends'.

The Globe Theatre and other theatres of the time used very little in the way of scenery and stage furnishings. There were no lighting effects as performances were held in daylight. The language therefore had to do the work of awakening the imagination, leading to highly descriptive passages and constant references to times of day and the state of the weather. There were no intervals, and the audience would come and go at will, would talk, both to the actors and each other, and would conduct all sorts of business while the play was going on. This explains the repetition in Shakespeare; he keeps you reminded of the plot so far, in case you missed some. Puck's speech at the start of Act III Scene ii for example gives no new information, though it is a joyous rendition of what has al-

The play

The fact that he never wrote another play in this form suggests again a lack of favour at the time – he was after all writing to please both the court of Queen Elizabeth (reigned 1558–1603; he compliments her specifically at Act II, scene i, line 157) and the groundlings (the holders of cheaper tickets who paid to stand) and was in the business of achieving continued success.

Until theatres were closed by Puritans in 1640, boy actors took on female roles. When they reopened in 1660, women began to act professionally.

Further study

Find out more about the form of entertainment known as 'masque' (although this is a very early example there are elements present in the play); the way fairies have been depicted through history; the character of Puck, or Robin Goodfellow, in traditional English fairy-tales; the story of Theseus and Hippolyta; the Globe and how plays were staged in Elizabethan times.

Staging

ready been observed. These days we would expect an audience to be listening and so either these repetitive passages are cut or, as in the case of Puck, we find ways of making the actual telling more exciting than what is being told.

Form

The play mingles poetry and prose throughout. There is a basic distinction applied to all Shakespeare's plays – that the court uses poetry and the lower orders use prose, and this is partially accurate. However, in Act V this is reversed deliberately during the Mechanicals performance to point out the humour of the interruptions and the relaxed nature of the members of the court after the triple wedding. This needs to be marked in performance.

It is important to understand Shakespeare's use of the iambic pentameter (five stressed syllables alternating with five unstressed ones), and how an actor will make use of it. Even when it sounds like natural speech, it is still poetry. The poetry cannot be ignored. An actor may make use of the stresses and, most importantly, the breaks in rhythm to help inform him of the intention behind the line. In this play there is also a great deal of rhyme that must be worked into the performance. Puck, for instance, can use his to find humour and entertainment value, whether for Oberon or the audience.

Further reading

If you want to look further into this aspect of Shakespearian acting then *Voice and the Actor* by Cicely Berry (Virgin 1993) is the best account of the actor's approach. Two good general texts on *A Midsummer Night's Dream* are *Shakespeare's Midsummer Night's Dream* ed. Antony Price (Macmillan 1983) and *Shakespeare in Production: A Midsummer Night's Dream* ed. Trevor Griffiths (Cambridge University Press 1996).

Volpone

Private theatres

Shakespeare's younger contemporary Ben Jonson was writing plays around the turn of the 17th century, at the time of the rise of the private theatre in London. This came about due to the uncertainty of the political future in the last years of Elizabeth's reign. James Burbage converted Blackfriars monastery into an indoor theatre in 1596 and set up a professional children's company there to great financial success. This led to further private theatres being built. The private theatre was smaller, more expensive and completely covered over. There was no great change in performance methods from those employed in the public theatres, but as they were indoors, artificial lighting was used for the first time, and there was a chance to experiment with the use of scenery. During Elizabeth's last years the political unrest and darkening mood led to the rise of a group of men who sought to express themselves through satire, and who developed a drama of social errors and vices. They were anti-romantic and looked for social criticism in their work. The drama became more concerned with the bourgeoisie – the middle-classes – rather than the court. Ben Jonson was the leader in this field.

The arrival of the Tudor dynasty in 1485 had brought years of civil war to an end. Elizabeth I had no obvious heir and the fear was that the death of the last Tudor might bring a return to civil war.

Image of the times

In the prologue to *Every Man in his Humour*, his first play, Jonson states his case for a more 'realistic' drama and puts down Shakespeare's history plays in which 'a child, now swaddled to proceed Man/And then shoot up, in one beard and weed/Past threescore years'. He hoped his audience '...will be pleased to see/One such to-day as other plays should be/Where neither chorus wafts you o'er the seas/Nor creaking throne comes down the boys to please' but rather 'deeds and language such as men do use/And persons such as comedy would choose/When she would show an image of the times'. That last phrase says it all – an image of the times. Jonson is satirising the very people who are likely to watch his plays. He wishes to comment on the errors of the age. He uses a 'scientific' form of approach to his characters, relating them to the 'humours'. This refers to the widely accepted medical opinion of the time that there were four basic 'humours', which in the well-balanced individual appeared in equal measures, but when unbalanced would cause disease. The four humours were: choler, melancholy, phlegm and blood. Jonson uses these four to create 'types' of characters – the testy old father, the melancholic miser, the bombastic soldier or the jealous husband, in each of which one of the humours is predominant. His dialogue is stinging and witty, but many would say the flaw of his writing is that there is no positive vision to counterbalance his society of diseased individuals: it is all negative, there are no sympathetic characters of any weight. In *Volpone*, written in 1606, the bestial characters (with appropriate animal names) are creatures born of a nightmare. However, as a terrible indictment of human greed and lust they give great scope for actors and designers, and this might explain why the play is still so popular today.

The play is a biting satire on human greed and as such is still relevant to modern audiences despite the difficulty of some of the language. Volpone, the fox, cons the richest and greediest members of Venetian society out of their wealth by promising them much from his will and by pretending to be on his deathbed, but receives his comeuppance at the hands of his own servant Mosca, the fly. Venice was considered the most affluent and corrupt city in renaissance Europe, and thus makes a perfect background for the story. The use of animals to underpin the characters gives the play the quality of a fable, and though it is a comedy, it does not end with a wedding but the censoring of all characters.

The Changeling

The Changeling, written by Thomas Middleton in 1622, is one of the last plays of the Jacobean age, which saw the growth and pinnacle of the great tragedies of English drama. Renaissance tragedy is based on Aristotelian tragedy in that it picks up on the idea of the tragic flaw, but in addition includes subplots and comic interludes to provide relief for the audience from the steady downfall of the major characters. Seneca (c. 3 BCE–65 CE) wrote a number of Latin adaptations of Greek tragedy and added elements that reappear in later tragedies, such as ghosts, a revenge element and resounding rhetorical speeches. From Senecan tragedy come the ghosts, violent and bloody deeds, and a five-act structure.

The Spanish Tragedy (c. 1587) by Thomas Kyd and works by Christopher Marlowe started the fashion in England for the revenge form of tragedy. Shakespeare's great tragedies appeared at the start of the 17th century: *Hamlet* in 1601, *Othello*, *King Lear* and *Macbeth* following swiftly thereafter. The political uncertainty of the era, and its bitterness and melancholic sentiment are reflected in these great dramatic works, and unlike Jonson who was reflecting merely the times in which he lived, these plays reflect the eternal questions of life: Who am I? Why am I? and What am I here for?

Not much is known of Middleton and co-author William Rowley. Middleton was the city chronologer from 1620 until his death when

Further study
Study the various animals that are personified in the play to understand their movement and manner and why they are appropriate to the characters. Consider the use of masks, and the purpose of satire in drama.

The play

Further reading
Try *Jonson: Volpone, a casebook* ed. Jonas Barish (Macmillan 1972).

Tragedy

For more on Aristotle and tragedy, see page 20.

Further reading
Try *Three Jacobean Revenge Tragedies* ed. R.V. Holdsworth (Macmillan 1990).

The play

Attribution in Jacobean plays is often complicated. Even though Rowley collaborated with Middleton on *The Changeling*, it is Middleton who is usually acknowledged as the author, Rowley being regarded as a sub-contractor on the job, so to speak.

Further study

Find out more about: revenge tragedy; the staging of ghosts through theatrical history; asylums in the Jacobean age.

Realism

he was succeeded by Jonson, and it is thought Rowley was an actor who helped others to revise plays, hence his collaborations with Middleton. Middleton's early plays were vicious comedies such as *A Chaste Maid in Cheapside*, but his later plays are nearly all collaborations, many with Rowley, from whom it is thought he gained his use of more serious and passionate verse structure. *The Changeling* marks the high point in their collaboration and the shared development of the character of De Flores produces one of the great villains of the period. The play's secondary plot, from which it takes its title, is less convincing, but provides much opportunity for the exploration of madness, which had been one of the main themes of the Jacobean period. Unlike the earlier revenge tragedies, crime here is born of crime, as in *Macbeth*. Beatrice's hiring of De Flores to commit murder for her leads to his physical demands of her, to which she succumbs with loathing, but finds that evil has penetrated her soul and so brings about her own end.

Three Sisters

Realism in the theatre can be considered to be the artistic reproduction of life on stage; as honest and objective a portrayal of human activity as is possible within the confines of theatrical endeavour. Realist artists try to keep their preconceived notions out of their work; they merely report what they see. Realism began as an artistic movement in the 19th century in Europe and included painting and literature as well as drama.

In drama, realism began as a means to make the theatre more socially useful. Popular and mainstream theatre in the latter half of the 19th century was mostly concerned with melodrama and comic opera, but various social revolutions and political reforms in Europe paved the way for change. In addition, the rise of modern science, with its emphasis on the observation and accurate recording of natural events, pushed realism to the fore. Charles Darwin's *On the Origin of the Species* (1859) shattered beliefs about the emergence of mankind by suggesting that all life developed from a common ancestry, controlled by environment. Humans were just another part of nature and not superior to everything else. This was, of course, in direct conflict with the Christian worldview. Equally, Karl Marx's doctrines concerning an equal distribution of wealth were taken on board by many artists, and this allowed for a drama which was not just about the higher social classes and was in fact actively against a class structure. Art was seen as a means to better mankind and it was thought this could be best achieved through realism.

Drama began to deal with contemporary settings and time periods, the problems of contemporary life and the common man rather than the court and high social classes of earlier drama. It was not widely popular due to the subject matters of poverty and disease, which were not felt to be appropriate for the theatre by many, and so realism took many years to become accepted. The movement began in France in literature with such writers as Alexandre Dumas (1824–1895) and Emile Augier (1820–1889) who kept a strict moral code in their writing; but the real father of realist drama is considered to be Henrik Ibsen (1828–1906), writing in Norway. His plays attack society's values through the medium of the 'well-made play'.

By using this form of writing he was able to make the shocking content of his plays more acceptable, though a number were banned in some countries for many years. His plays emphasised psychological motivation of character. The social environment was seen to heavily influence a character's behaviour.

Anton Chekhov's (1860–1904) use of realism is perhaps more poetic than Ibsen. He takes realism to its extremes, to the point where his plays are often criticised for having no plot at all. Characters merely exist; they seem trapped in their social environment, living with hope in a hopeless situation. The plot of *Three Sisters* has been summed up as: 'Three sisters keep saying they will go to Moscow – they never do – the end'! But this is to deny the plays their subtexts. We understand more about these characters from what is not said than what is. Chekhov described it thus: 'On the stage everything should be as complex and as simple as in life. People are eating their dinner, just eating their dinner, and while they're eating it, their future happiness is being decided or their lives are about to be shattered.' It was not until Konstantin Stanislavski (1863–1938) that Chekhov's plays found an audience; and this was because Stanislavski allowed the actors to develop their characters with depth of understanding through realism. Chekhov was not pleased with Stanislavski's productions of his plays as he felt he was writing comic satire rather than the tragedies Stanislavski turned them into. However, the two forms can sit happily together and have often done so very successfully in 20th-century productions.

The play has as a central theme the frustration with provincial life as experienced by the four children of the deceased General Prozorov. Each of them is disappointed in love and is dissatisfied with their working lives. They seem to feel that a return to Moscow would make all their problems disappear. They live in hope of a better future, but seem unable to make this future happen. It may be that they don't go to Moscow because they are afraid that they will be proved wrong in their hopes if they do. The play has the potential of tragedy, but we are also amused by the banalities of their lives. We are left at the end with a sense of lives being unfulfilled and thus reflect upon our own existence.

The Shadow of a Gunman

Sean O'Casey (1880–1964) was born into a Protestant family living in a grim tenement in the Dublin slums. He suffered from poor eyesight all his life, which kept him out of school for long periods of time, but this did not restrict his passionate need to learn. He was an idealist who had a strong sense of justice. O'Casey became involved with the Gaelic League (see *below*) and with amateur theatre early in his life and found his faith in the socialist ideals of Jim Larkin's crusade for the Irish working class that began with the general strike of 1913. In order to fully appreciate the setting and background for *The Shadow of a Gunman*, which is set in 1920, there is a need to understand the background of the Irish civil war.

On 24 April 1916, Easter Monday, 1,600 Irish nationalists launched the Easter Rising to fight for an independent Ireland. There are many different reasons why some of the nationalist organisations felt the

Ibsen's play *Ghosts*, with its revelations of a family destroyed by debauchery and syphilis, and its thoughts on euthanasia, is a prime example.

Chekhov

Further study

Find out more about: 20th-century Russian history, including the rise of the revolutionaries and the position of the landowners and the bourgeoisie; the original productions of *The Seagull* in St Petersburg and in Moscow; the Moscow Arts Theatre; Konstantin Stanislavski.

See pages 102–117 for more on Stanislavski.

The play

Further reading

Try *Anton Chekhov* by Laurence Senelick (Macmillan 1985) or *File on Chekhov* ed. Nick Warrall (Methuen 1986).

The Easter Rising

Web Link

For a timeline of important events leading up to the Easter Risings, go to http://indigo.ie/~1916/timeline.html

need for an armed insurrection. Perhaps a major reason was the famine – or Great Hunger – of the 1840s (when 1,000,000 people died of starvation). The massive emigration that followed convinced many that the British government was effectively pursuing a policy of land clearance, which many saw as resulting in the decline of the Irish language and culture. This suspicion fuelled a renewed move towards independence. When the rising came it led to a six-day battle – during which much of Dublin city centre was destroyed. The executions of the leaders of the uprising by British authorities increased support for the nationalists in Ireland, but the disputed moves to independence resulted in civil war.

The play

The Shadow of a Gunman was first presented by the Abbey Theatre in Dublin in 1923 and was the first of what became a trio of like-minded plays (along with *Juno and the Paycock* and *The Plough and the Stars*) that are similar in theme and technique and are often said to form a tragi-comic trilogy. These are all pacifist plays in which the main characters are not national heroes actually engaged in the fighting, but are the non-combatants in a city under military siege. The background to *The Shadow of a Gunman* is the guerrilla warfare between the rebellious Irish Republican Army (IRA) and the British forces, consisting mainly of the ruthless auxiliary troops known as the Black and Tans. In the play a poet and a pedlar become caught up in the war. Donal Davoren, the poet, is mistaken by those in the tenement as a member of the IRA on the run and he encourages the deception, particularly with the impressionable Minnie, which leads to her downfall. Deception is a major theme in the play. Donal is deceiving himself and others, and is not even a good poet. He is a 'shadow' of a poet as much as he is a 'shadow' of a gunman and it takes the shock of Minnie's death for him to see himself with clarity. Seamas, the pedlar, understands the chaos in which he lives; he knows that poetry and patriotic poses will not help, but is too lazy to do anything about it. He merely takes to his bed when trouble comes his way.

The first productions of these three plays provoked a public outcry because of O'Casey's consistent refusal to paint a patriotic picture or to glorify the violence of the nationalist movement, instead presenting the message that the deaths of innocent people far outnumbered the deaths of heroes.

Yerma

Lorca

Federico García Lorca (1898–1936) was born in a small village in the countryside around Granada, southern Spain, the son of a prosperous farmer and his second wife, who had been a schoolteacher. Vincenta Lorca Romero was an independent and cultured woman who loved music and literature and who held great influence over her son. The rural nature of his upbringing was hugely important to Lorca (later in life he remarked, 'my most distant childhood memories have the taste of earth in them') and this is clearly apparent in all his major works. He was a poet, musician and playwright with a passion for the Spanish folk ballads and traditions of his youth. At university he read law, but at the same time studied music under Manuel de Falla, becoming an expert guitarist and piano player. He also worked with Salvador Dali and the film director

Further study

Find out more about: the Abbey Theatre, Dublin, and the original production; the Nationalist movement; life in the tenement slums of Dublin in 1920.

Further reading

Try *File on O'Casey* by Nesta Jones (Methuen 1986) and *O'Casey: the Dublin Trilogy* ed. Ronald Ayling (Macmillan 1985).

At the first performances of *The Shadow of a Gunman*, warning notices had to be posted about the loud gunfire and off-stage noises of the raid in the second act in order to reassure the audience that these were not real noises from outside the theatre, as the raids were still very much a part of every day life.

Federico Lorca, *Obras completas* vol 2 (Galaxia Gutenberg 1999).

Louis Bunuel, though he fell out with both after they made a short film, *Un Chien Andalou*, which he thought to be about him. He became well known for his recitations of his own poetry and by 1928 he was the best known of all Spanish poets and the leading member of the 'Generation of 27'.

Lorca lived for a short time in New York, but found the cultural change shocking, and returned to Spain via Cuba. He ran a theatre company, La Barraca, which toured classical plays to the provinces. *Blood Wedding*, the first of what was supposed to be a trio of rural plays, was performed in 1933. *Yerma* followed in 1934. He never completed the trilogy, as although *The House of Bernarda Alba* was written just before his death in 1936, it was not part of the trilogy. The Spanish Civil War began in 1936 and Lorca was an early casualty. As an intellectual (and very likely left wing and homosexual) he was considered dangerous by Franco's Nationalists and early on the morning of 19 August he was shot and buried in an unmarked grave that he had been forced to dig for himself. He had recently remarked to a journalist: 'I am still learning my profession. My work has just begun.'

Further reading

Try *Federico García Lorca* by Reed Anderson (Macmillan 1984).

Theatre in Spain in the 1910s and 1920s was in a strange position. Commercially successful productions of witty middle-class comedies and tragi-comedies held sway, although there was constant discussion among the critics that theatre was in a crisis due to the fact that serious or political works could not find an audience, despite the efforts of many of the young dramatists of the day. In Madrid there was one arts theatre, the Teatro Eslava, which cultivated talented, young scenic artists and playwrights. It was unique in producing international works alongside those by new Spanish writers. It brought works by Ibsen, Shaw and Barrie to the Spanish people and in 1920 introduced Lorca's ill-fated play *Butterfly's Evil Spell* to the stage. This was a fanciful and highly poetic play, which closed after only one performance. Lorca continued to speak passionately about the theatre through a series of lectures; at the heart of his efforts to revolutionise theatre was his belief that great drama had always been poetic drama. He also felt strongly that theatre should show people the truth about their lives. He appreciated the problems inherent in a commercially based theatre, but looked to reinstate a theatre that challenged its audience by asking moral questions. Lorca felt that a rural audience could be rediscovered if presented with imaginative and disciplined theatre, and so his travelling company was founded, which tested its audience with a repertoire of classic plays produced in both fully staged and minimalist productions, and thus, in his words, 'revived their culture'. He wanted art that was accessible to all. The experiment, which he added to by starting theatre clubs in the cities dedicated to producing for free the plays the commercial managements would not touch, was remarkably successful. By doing this Lorca was continuing the best tradition of theatre, which seeks to nurture the best of new, young talent and at the same time educates audiences in contemporary production methods.

Theatre in Spain

Further study

Find out more about: Spanish theatre history; the political history of Spain in the 1920s and 1930s, including the rise of Franco; symbolism and surrealism in art; Andalusia, its customs, people and climate.

Yerma tells the tragedy of a woman trapped in a loveless and sterile marriage, unable to conform to the traditions and social attitudes of her society. Longing for the baby her husband is not interested in

The play

giving her, Yerma is drawn to another man, but is prevented from going to him by her own conscience and the social conventions of honour. Yerma, driven by longing and frustration eventually murders her husband. The play is a piece of writing full of symbolism (even the name Yerma is not real, but means 'barren' or 'empty' as applied to land), with an emphasis on the cyclical aspects of Man and Nature. Using lyricism, music and song, the play needs to be treated as a tragic poem in performance.

Restoration

Royal Court Theatre

Edward Bond is a playwright who is inextricably linked to the Royal Court Theatre. This theatre has been the home of modern, radical playwrights since World War II, and it is from here that the new waves of political and social drama have spread out across Britain. After the war it was recognised by some that British theatre was, in director Peter Brook's words, 'deadly theatre' – the kind of theatre that appealed to the middle classes only, in that it presented them with bourgeois comedies and safe revivals of classic plays. George Devine, the first director of the Court, wanted a theatre that produced 'popular art' aimed at all. One of the earliest plays produced at the Court was the groundbreaking *Look Back in Anger* by John Osborne, which began the reign of the 'angry young men', including Wesker and Arden. They wrote plays about real people doing real things in real situations. At the same time the Court was also doing productions of plays by European playwrights such as Ionesco, Genet and Brecht.

> **Web link**
>
> Read all about the Royal Court Theatre at www.royalcourttheatre.com.

Bond

Edward Bond, who was born in 1934, presented his first play to the Court in 1962. *A Pope's Wedding* was given a single 'production without decor' and led to him having a new play commissioned. This turned out to be the notorious *Saved*, a play that caused great controversy. The play was banned by the then Lord Chamberlain – who held the right of censorship of the theatre at the time – due to its bad language and an infamous scene wherein young lads stone a baby in its pram. But the Royal Court, defending the right of a play to be shown as it was written, turned itself temporarily into a club theatre in order to stage the play in 1965. The critics were generally horrified by the content of the play. Bond's brutal, uncompromising scenes of south-London thuggery asked questions about the nature of theatre. Had theatre the right to shock if as a result important debates were opened up about contemporary life? Clearly Bond thinks so, and his plays have continued to ask this question. He is renowned for his use of violence on stage, for example in *Lear* (his reworking of *King Lear*).

In this he has inspired a generation of writers, most notably the late Sarah Kane, whose work, *Blasted*, received much the same critical mauling as *Saved* had done thirty years before.

Socio-political concerns

Bond is a socio-political writer, and uses elements of the epic theatre of the German playwright Bertolt Brecht (1898–1956) in order to demand questions of his audience. His plays are often constructed from a series of short scenes (montage) that are not necessarily chronological. He uses music and song in much the same way as Brecht did. He shares Brecht's Marxist views and uses historical references throughout his work. Like Brecht, he often adapts the work of previous dramatists (such as Chekhov and Shakespeare) and makes use of past theatrical forms such as the parable play, Greek myths, epic theatre, European forms of theatre and Restora-

Brecht uses music and song to comment on the action of the play, to act as a counterpoint to the story and give it a contemporary social context, allowing the audience to make these connections and see the relevance of historical issues to modern society.

tion comedy, as in *Restoration*, to comment on contemporary society. He stated in an interview in 2000 that it should be theatre's role 'to recreate what it means to be human, to redefine our relationship with the world', *The Guardian*, 05/04/00. Bond is now rarely performed in Britain, but his plays are often produced in Europe and he receives much more praise there than here as he is so vociferous in his feelings about the political climate of this country. In the same interview he also stated: 'The Comédie Française says I'm the most important theoretician of drama since Brecht. Well, it's a fact.' Bond's new work is more likely to be performed by theatre-in-education groups, as he is more interested in engaging a child in drama than an adult, arguing that a child is more enthusiastic and more open to change. In the classroom, he claims, his drama can have a more imaginative effect.

Restoration was produced in 1981, directed by the playwright. Set in 18th-century England, in a world of cruelty and injustice, Lord Are casually murders his wife (whom he married for money) over the breakfast table and seeks to pin the murder on his illiterate footman Bob Hedges, who is an avid supporter of his master. The play is therefore about injustice, particularly in relation to class, but it uses its historical setting to comment on the modern world (1980s) by looking at other divisions in society: town against country, black against white, old against young. In an article in *The Guardian* in 1981, Bond himself describes the play as being about the betrayal of the working class Tory voter, and the relationship between this and racial conflict. 'Violent confrontation is inevitable if you are forced to live irrationally. Because it is the only way things will change.'

Further reading

Try *Bond on file* ed. Philip Roberts (Methuen 1985) or *Edward Bond* by David L. Hurst (Macmillan 1985).

The play

Further study

Find out more about: the Restoration period, both history and the theatre; the political climate in England in the late 1970s; the rise of Thatcherism; Brecht; Bond's use of poetry.

The actor's approach

When you come to answer an examination question on an actor's approach to a text you **must** answer from the performance perspective. This is true of the director and designer too, but in the case of the actor you might be misled by the word 'approach' into thinking that you are being asked to write about rehearsal methods. The particular danger is that you may confuse this section of the exam with that on the practitioners and write about process: for example, if you have studied Stanislavski then you should NOT be discussing how you would use his idea of emotion memory when playing Masha in *Three Sisters*. Within this section we may well refer to rehearsal process, but in the examination you are asked to write on the result of that process, the product if you like. The questions are always in the form of 'how would you perform the role of…', not 'how would you prepare the role of…'. It is very important to understand the difference and not to confuse the two.

Note that in the examination your gender is irrelevant. If the character you are asked to write about is male and you are female, don't be concerned with discussing how you will change your own physicality and characteristics in order to portray a man. This will send you down a blind alley. Just assume that you are a man, or vice versa. The important thing is that you are explaining how *as an actor* you will perform the role.

Character

Which role?

The first reading of your set text that you did at the start of this chapter should have thrown up some immediate reactions to some of the characters, and, if you are an actor, you may have found you had a desire to play one or two of them more than the others. However, for the purposes of the examination you must be prepared to write on any of the characters; you will not be given a choice. So how should you work on the play, not knowing which role you will be cast in until you get into the examination? The answer is to work on a number of roles in the play in some detail and, because the approach is the same in each case, if a different role comes up you will be able to work through the formula quite readily. The approach we suggest should work for any role in any of the eight plays and will cover the aspects that are being looked for in your response.

Go with your first impressions. You may well change your mind later and that is fine; for an actor that is the point of rehearsals, to find out what works and what doesn't.

By this stage you will have read the play, made your first-impression notes and done some research, which may well have answered some of your initial questions. Having chosen a particular role to work on from an actor's point of view you should now re-read the play with particular reference to that character. Assess how the character fits into the main pattern of the play and try to find the responses to the following list of quite general questions:

➢ What appears to be the main reason your character is in the play?

➢ Is the character the main focus, part of the main plot or involved in the subplot?

➢ Does the character lead the action or are they affected by the action?

➢ Is the character basically a 'good guy' or a 'bad guy'?

➢ What picture comes to mind as you think about the character?

➢ Which scenes are you excited by the prospect of acting?

➢ Which scenes seem boring, or worry you? (These will be the scenes that as an actor you would probably spend the most time on.)

Character research

See the sections *above* for information on each play.

You may need to do detailed research on the character, depending upon the play and role. Areas for research might include: historical period (facts, manners, costume, real events, style of living etc.); cultural differences (country of setting, attitudes, beliefs etc.); accents or dialects; performance styles. Adapt these areas of research for your chosen character.

Character background

Establish the background of your character with the help of the questions set out below. Find the answers from the text of the play and add your imaginative extension afterwards.

Start by finding out the given circumstances for your character by answering these questions as if you were them:

See page 105 for more on the given circumstances.

➢ What era is the play set in?

➢ What location? Country? The actual set or sets, the imagined off-stage rooms, the places I work in etc.?

➢ What time of year is it?

- ➤ What time of day is it?
- ➤ What is the weather like?
- ➤ What is my name, age, class, job?
- ➤ Where do I live?
- ➤ What sort of family, relations, friends do I have?
- ➤ How well off am I?
- ➤ Are there any dominating physical characteristics caused by age, wealth, health or social conditions?
- ➤ What is my taste in clothes, music, art, theatre, cinema, books and sport?
- ➤ Have I an overwhelming purpose in my life?
- ➤ Have I a dominant quality in my character?
- ➤ What is said about me in the play: by myself, to my face, behind my back?
- ➤ What are my reactions to other characters in the play?
- ➤ What briefly is my past history?
- ➤ What would an average day be like in detail?
- ➤ Do I have an accent or dialect? (If the answer is yes this will probably lead to further study.)

Having got the answers to these general questions you will now have built up a great deal of information about your character, a blueprint if you like, which will form the basis of the practical work to follow. You will even have the answers to some thoughts about the physicality and vocal characteristics of your role, which we will look at in more detail shortly.

You should now start to look at each scene in the play and ask some specific questions in order to understand your character's motivation and purpose. Begin with your entrances and exits, which are often the most telling part of any scene and therefore vital for an actor to get right. The moment you walk on stage the audience will start to make judgements about your character, and thus you must know the answers to the following questions:

Entrances

- ➤ Why am I entering? What is my objective?
- ➤ What has occurred from my point of view since the last entrance I made, and how does this affect the way I am acting?
- ➤ Where have I come from?
- ➤ What mood am I in?
- ➤ Do I know the room/space I am entering?
- ➤ Do I know if there is anyone in the room/space?
- ➤ Do I know the people in the room/space and what is my attitude towards them?

Exits

- ➤ Why am I leaving?
- ➤ Where am I going to?
- ➤ What mood am I in?

Character motivation

Think about…

The entrance of Masha and Vershinin into Act II of *Three Sisters*. They enter mid-conversation with Masha saying 'I don't know'. By answering these questions you will have a much better idea of what the characters are feeling and thinking about as they enter the room.

Think about…

Helena's exit at the end of Act I Scene i of *A Midsummer Night's Dream*. The answers to these questions may make her run from the stage in a much more positive mood than that with which she entered the scene.

➢ Am I going far away or somewhere close by?

➢ Have I achieved the purpose for which I entered?

You must be certain of your objective in each scene. The action of the play may well change your objective during each scene, but you must always be clear about what your character wants to achieve. As a simple example your objective might be 'I want to sit in the armchair and go to sleep', but as you move to the armchair the phone rings and while your main objective stays the same, your secondary objective becomes 'I must answer the phone'.

The more you work on the character the closer you will look at each line the character speaks. Find out what sentence is important in each scene and what words are important in each sentence. This will prevent you from falling into the trap of giving too much emphasis to everything you say, thus missing light and shade. Clarity of thought in all you say is essential, but you need to select what is important and what requires emphasis. So:

➢ Decide to whom you are saying each line, and which lines are virtually to yourself as an expression of your thoughts

➢ Are any lines said to the audience? If so, are they said directly to them or are they merely a voicing of your thoughts to the world?

➢ You must understand the meaning, purpose and therefore the feeling of every line you speak

➢ You must know why one line follows another – if there appears to be a complete break or change of thought you must find a reason for it. On stage as in life you must have continuity of thought

➢ You must speak your lines with belief in order to make the other characters understand what you are trying to convey to them, and you must listen to other characters' lines intently (really listen, not just giving the impression of listening) until you logically answer with your next line.

This is a very detailed process and one that a professional actor would use when working on a role, but it should work equally well for any role in any of the eight set plays. By this stage you should have a thorough knowledge of your character and will begin to understand what motivates them.

We are now going to look at the various aspects of characterisation that are given in the specification and which will be looked for in your answers.

Physical qualities

The first thing an audience can respond to (and remember that everything is really about gaining the appropriate audience response) when your character walks on stage is the visual impression you make, so a good starting point is to discuss what you think the character should look like. What shape will you be? What height? What facial features? The examiner has no idea what you look like, so don't be afraid to suggest the look you wish to have for the chosen character. Always remember though that all visual qualities must be related to your interpretation of the character.

See the section on Stanislavski for more on this.

Think about…

How will you say lines when you are the only character on stage, as in Helena's speech in the example mentioned above? Are they to yourself or direct to the audience? These moments are called soliloquies and need special consideration.

Think about…

Asides are lines spoken to yourself or to the audience when there are other characters on stage who do not hear what you say. These too need special attention. Think about the constant use of asides in *The Changeling* and how you will deal with them.

Appearance

Further reading

Any books or articles written by actors on their work are useful. Well worth reading are: *Year of the King* by Anthony Sher (Methuen 1985) and the three-book series Players of Shakespeare (Cambridge University Press 1988).

For instance you may decide that Lord Are in *Restoration* should be a short but large-stomached, well-fed man with a round, red face and bushy sideburns. This is fine, but remember that all decisions must be justified, so your essay might read:

> I would play Lord Are as a short man, with a large stomach, a round, red face and bushy sideburns. The roundness of the character will suggest a well-fed man, who has a relatively easy life with servants who do everything for him. I would use the fact that I am short and make sure taller and thinner actors played the servants so that I might appear somewhat ridiculous when standing near them. The red face will suggest a man who likes his drink and the country air, and the sideburns are a feature of the restoration period in which the play is set and will suggest a vanity within the character.

Part of the initial impression is clearly given by the costume a character is wearing when they first enter; and although this would normally be chosen by the designer, it is perfectly acceptable for you to mention as the actor what you think you should be wearing, and, often more importantly, how you will be wearing it. Thus you should make reference to your choices of costume and make-up or mask, if any, in brief detail, showing how this relates to your interpretation of the character and what it will show to your audience as a first impression. For example, as the character of Volpone in his opening scenes you might wish to state:

> I will be wearing dark red silk pyjamas with a voluminous furry dressing-gown, which has a long cord attached that stretches down behind in the manner of a tail, a long wig of slicked-back red hair, large mutton chop sideburns in a similar colour and a false pointed nose, all with the intention of suggesting the vulpine nature of the character to the audience immediately, while at the same time emphasising his wealth and love of fine things. I will keep folding the dressing gown around my body and stroking its fur in a manner to show my pleasure and enjoyment of the fun to come.

Some playwrights give you no indication of the look of a character, as in the case of Lord Are above; others give you a few indications within the text (we know for instance that Helena must be taller than Hermia in *A Midsummer Night's Dream*) whereas others give a very clear indication of what the character should look like. Sean O'Casey, for instance, gives very precise instructions within the stage directions for his characters in *The Shadow of a Gunman*. However, it is entirely up to the director and actor whether these are followed through, and thus up to you as you make your decisions. Take for example Mrs Grigson in *The Shadow of a Gunman*. O'Casey's description runs as follows:

> She is a woman of 40, but looks much older. She is one of the cave dwellers of Dublin, living as she does in a tenement kitchen, to which only the occasional sickly beam of sunlight filters through a grating in the yard; the consequent general dimness of her abode has given her a habit of peering through half-closed eyes. She is slovenly dressed in an old skirt and bodice; her face is grimy, not because her habits are dirty – for, although she is untidy, she is a clean woman – but because of the smoky atmosphere of her room. Her hair is constantly falling over her face, which she is as frequently removing by rapid movements of her right hand.

For more detailed exploration of the use of costume, make-up and masks, see the section on the designer's approach, page 76.

Practical exercise

Try wearing a coat in different ways: over your shoulder, tied up tightly, held over your arms or unbuttoned and loose. What might these different positions suggest about your mood? It is quite useful to do this sort of exercise in front of a mirror.

It would be perhaps foolish to go completely against this as so much of the character is given in these directions. Equally there would be no point in merely reproducing all of this in your essay, as you will not be credited for copying. However, you could make use of this information by referring to the significant points and suggesting ways of establishing them on stage in your performance, perhaps as follows:

> I would show Mrs Grigson to seem older than her years, as O'Casey suggests, by walking slowly with a slight stoop in my posture, by emphasising the lines on my face through make-up and by doing nothing to show the femininity of my body. The slight stoop will suggest the weariness of the hard working wife. I would peer 'through half-closed eyes' at the other characters, especially those in whose presence I might feel nervous, such as Davoren. I would wear clean but well-worn clothing, though my hands and face would appear grimy to show the 'smoky atmosphere' in which she lives. I would have long, somewhat unkempt hair, which I would keep tucking behind my ears in a seemingly automatic gesture to show that it is a common occurrence and one which she is relatively unaware of doing.

Movement

The next stage is to think about how the character should move in order to reveal certain characteristics to the audience. You will need to be aware of the way an actor changes their movement in order to express different aspects of their character. One area for consideration should be the way you walk, your gait. What is going to be the length of your stride for instance? Will your walk be light or heavy-footed? Will your body have a sway to it or be quite rigid as you move?

With your chosen text try to find appropriate walks for the various characters. Actors often state that once they have found the right shoes for their character, they can really start to find the inner character. This is because one of the most individual things about us is the way we walk.

Another area to consider is posture: the stance of your character. In the example above, we suggested Mrs Grigson was stooped to show weariness, but some characters might be straight-backed, or stand with a slight lean. Try different postures yourself and see what they suggest about you to an observer. Be careful of over-exaggerating, you may wish to be quite subtle in your use of posture, though for rehearsal purposes it is often useful to extend each aspect further to see just how far you can go before it becomes ludicrous or clichéd. Think also about the use of gesture. Watch the way people around you use their hands when speaking. Some people are highly expressive and their hands are in constant movement, whereas others hardly make use of them, or keep them firmly in pockets. Gesture is often indicative of background, especially nationality, so consider this when preparing your character. But also be aware of how much this can say about an individual character. For example, De Flores in *The Changeling* might use his hands to show his lust for Beatrice, by rubbing them together constantly while watching her, or, rather more unpleasantly, stroking his own face and body with outstretched fingers.

Practical exercise

Try walking with different parts of your body leading the way. What difference does it make for instance if you lead from your nose or your groin? You will probably find that the former is more suitable for an inquisitive type of person, while the latter suggests a more confident, sexually-aware character.

Practical exercise

Try to incorporate specific animal movements in your walk. It is often holpful to assign a suitable animal to a character and make use of the appropriate movement as a starting point in your exploration of character. You might feel, for example, that Titania has cat-like qualities; how could this idea help your movement?

Practical exercise

Try expressing different moods and thoughts to a colleague merely through the use of your hands, not in the sense of mime, but through gesture alone.

Of course characters will change their gait, stance and use of gesture depending on the situation they are in, just as we do in real life, but there will be certain aspects of each that are a part of their general nature. You will, when writing about a certain moment for a character, be more specific about movement, and we will look at this a little later.

Vocal qualities

Having considered physical movement, think about how you use your voice, especially volume, pitch, pace, use of pauses, tone and accent. All these need to be understood and explored in a practical manner whatever role you are considering.

Volume clearly refers to the level of sound produced by a character. Are they a loud or softly-spoken person and what does this suggest about them? Although we all vary the level of our voices, you should think about the midpoint of a person's sound level. A military man, for instance, might have a loud bark whereas a nervous woman might only just be audible. Remember though that projection will always be important, as those in the back row of your auditorium must be able to hear you. However, it is still possible to speak quietly and project your voice – this is part of an actor's training and is more a matter of correct breathing methods than volume. Think too about the importance of specific moments here; if a normally gently-spoken person suddenly explodes and shouts, this says far more about their mood at that moment than when a loud person shouts. Make use of extremes and changes to make points about the personality of the character.

Pitch is to do with the height or depth of a voice. Think of it in musical terms where it refers to the note that is being played. Most people use a very small pitch range while speaking; the very worst being those we call monotonous because they rarely move off one pitch. Good public speakers use a wide pitch range – listen to passionate politicians. Actors explore the range of their voices extensively in order to grab the audience's attention, but also to establish an overall pitch range for each character.

Pace is the speed at which a character talks. Try taking one of Puck's speeches from *A Midsummer Night's Dream* and performing it slowly, then at a more normal speed and then much faster. Which gives him more energy and excitement? Perhaps a specific pace will give him a more child-like feeling, or make him more devious. You will need to choose the one that best fits your interpretation, but clearly the pace will change the character quite significantly. The pace will also change from speech to speech (perhaps even within a speech) and should do so in order to indicate a shift of mood.

Making use of pauses can be very important when working on a character's speech patterns. Pause adds emphasis to what is being said. If you choose to pause for a significant amount of time in the middle of a sentence or before a specific word, then greater emphasis is added to that moment. You are suggesting, both to the character to whom you are speaking and to the audience, that what you are saying at that precise moment is important and should be taken

Volume

Think about...

How might Oberon use volume in *A Midsummer Night's Dream*? He gets angry with both Titania and Puck; who might he shout at more loudly?

Pitch

Practical exercise

In *Antigone* for example, would Antigone or Ismene have the deeper voice? Try it both ways and see which has the stronger effect.

Pace

See the section on tempo-rhythm on page 115 to explore the idea of pace still further.

Pause

note of. It can also suggest that a character is trying to find the correct words to describe their thoughts at that particular moment. Of course, as with all these elements, the use of pauses will then combine with the tone in which the following words are said to suggest a particular interpretation to the audience.

Tone

Tone is the mood or weight given to a phrase or section of text. This gives the text its atmosphere and is significant in showing the subtext of speech. Think of the phrase 'I could murder you'. If you were to say this in a light-hearted tone, with perhaps a laugh before, after or during the line, then the meaning will be significantly different from it being said slowly, with a slight pause before the word 'murder' and in a menacing tone of voice. The first is clearly meant jokingly, suggesting that you are slightly annoyed that someone has perhaps made a bit of a fool of you, whereas the latter suggests that you really would like to murder them. The context will help to make the intention clear, but you need to find the right tone of voice for the situation and your interpretation of the character.

Accent

Accent can either mean adding emphasis to a word or phrase, or something that indicates which country your character comes from. If your character is supposed to be Italian then you will need to decide whether you are going to use an Italian accent or not, which is likely to depend upon your director's interpretation of the play. Remember that accent is to do with the nationality and dialect is about regional variation. Thus Bottom from *A Midsummer Night's Dream* may have a Yorkshire dialect or a French accent.

Think about…

Which plays might need particular accents? Surely *The Shadow of a Gunman* needs Dublin accents and certainly Irish of some kind; *Yerma* might need an accent to suggest a location; you could use any accents in *A Midsummer Night's Dream* and indeed a combination of accents might aid the comedy.

Character relationships and use of space

You will need to think about the relationships your character has with others on stage and how, as an actor, you will show these relationships. For instance, if you are playing Natasha in her short scene at the end of Act I of *Three Sisters*, you will need to show her relationship with the rest of the household. Perhaps you have decided that she should be shown as something of an outsider, doing her best to fit in and be friendly with the rest, but becoming embarrassed rather easily, leading to her rushed exit from the ballroom and her moment with Andrey. The sort of things to consider are the way she uses the space. This is not her house yet, so you could make her seem uncomfortable and this can be shown by not appearing settled within the space or by moving around as if unsure where your rightful place in the room is. When you sit at the table with the others, will you sit comfortably or show awkwardness through a more rigid posture or even through constant movement on the chair?

Practical exercise

Try sitting in a chair in the following ways: to show it is your favourite, comfortable chair; to suggest discomfort; to show it was your father's chair; to show you are among friends; to show you are among strangers; to show fear.

In addition to the use of the furniture and environs of the space think also about your proximity to other characters. As Natasha you are given plenty of information to work with here. She kisses Irina in a 'vigorous and prolonged' manner and then kisses Olga when she enters, but how exactly will she do this? Perhaps she should embrace the sisters rather too tightly and falsely to show her nervousness, or perhaps with air-kisses that have little warmth behind them? This will depend on your interpretation of Natasha and how much you want to pre-empt the changes in her character that we see later in the play, which are perhaps suggested by the

Practical exercise

With a partner, enter the room to show the following relationships through physical contact and use of space: a long-married couple; two people who have not spoken to each other for years; newly weds; one is attracted to the other who is not interested.

fact that the first thing she does on entering the room is to examine herself in the mirror. This action can show a great deal about the character and needs careful thought – is it that she is the sort of person who cannot pass a mirror without checking her reflection and thus that the action is instinctive, or is it more deliberate than that, performed as a sign of her selfishness? Also the room is full of people she has not met before, so how will you reflect this? Will you catch their eyes or avoid looking at them in the face? How close will she allow herself to get to any of the other men in the room for example? These sorts of decisions will make a big difference in the way the character is perceived and would need to be written about in detail if discussing how you would perform this particular scene.

Sample question

A Midsummer Night's Dream
How would you perform the role of Bottom in Act I Scene ii, and what responses would you wish to gain from your audience?

Ideas for planning

- Start with your general interpretation of Bottom – his overall character and his function in the play. Is he there merely to create entertainment and make the audience laugh, or is there a more serious nature to him? Perhaps you see him as the professional actor's revenge on the amateur. Should there be a broad streak to the comedy making him a larger-than-life character or will you be looking for more subtle forms of humour? What response are you aiming for – laughter, irritation or sympathy, or perhaps a combination? This opening paragraph is setting out your intentions for the essay, but at the same time immediately giving a personal impression of how you would play Bottom. It is always advisable to write in the first person as that way your personality and individuality will come through the essay and you should remain focused.

- Next give your ideas for his initial appearance. What shape, build and look will you have? Include here personal details such as weight and height, and refer to any contrasts with the other characters. Will Bottom be much bigger than the other Mechanicals, for example? What costume will you be wearing and what does this say about your interpretation? What will be the state of your clothes – clean and pristine, or showing effects of work – is he a clean-faced man or slightly grubby? Will you be carrying anything – references to his profession for example?

- Discuss his physical characteristics – his posture, gait etc. Will you have any idiosyncrasies – particular gestures for example? Then his vocal qualities: what sort of voice will you use? Will it be a large booming voice or a more gentle sound? What accent or dialect might you have? Don't forget always to justify your choices by saying what you are trying to suggest to your audience.

- Look at the scene itself in detail. Choose moments from the scene and suggest how you will play them and in particular how you will show the relationships he has with the others. Does he mean to annoy Quince at the start of the scene or is he just eager and excited

A malapropism is the misuse of a word. The term comes from the character Mrs Malaprop in Sheridan's *The Rivals* where she notoriously misapplies words. For example, 'As headstrong as an allegory on the banks of the Nile'.

Further study

Useful books to help with understanding the director's approach are: *Playing Shakespeare* by John Barton (Methuen 1984), *A Director Calls* by Wendy Lesser (Faber 1997), *Women Directors on Directing* (Methuen 1999) and *Letters to George* by Max Stafford Clark (Nick Hern Books 1990).

In your 'virtual' productions of the set plays you do not have to be worried at all about costs. If you want to have a hydraulically controlled lift on stage or a chorus of 59 then have them, just make sure you are able to explain why you want them.

by the play and wanting to get on with it? Whereabouts on stage will you be in relation to the other characters? How will you perform the 'raging rocks' poem? What kinds of voice will he use for Thisbe and the other characters, and how will you change your own voice to suit these moments? Are there any moments of slapstick or physical humour in the scene – perhaps with props such as various coloured beards? Is he aware of the malapropisms he speaks or is the humour in the fact that some of the others are aware but he is not? With all of your ideas you should refer to the effect they will have on your audience and why you have chosen to perform the character in this way. The finer the detail you can give, the better. Discuss how individual lines should be spoken and performed. Remember that your intention is to make your interpretation and performance of the role extremely clear. The essay in a sense is a blueprint for another actor to read and be able to follow your ideas in practice.

The director's approach

The director is usually the person on a production team with the most decisions to make and with the most control over the production. The actors and designers, stage technicians and crew will all have to answer to the director.

Historically the role of the director is a relatively new one. In Shakespeare's time there was no one individual responsible for overseeing and controlling what the audience saw. Theatres put on vast repertoires of plays with minimal rehearsal time; there was no time for the luxury of a particular interpretation of any text. If anything this fell to the dramatist himself. One of the leading players may have taken responsibility for staging the play – the blocking – in order to prevent chaos on stage. This would include the timing of exits and entrances, and the grouping of characters on stage, but not how the actors played their roles. It was only in the middle of the 19th century that the prototype of the modern director came into being, and only in the last 50 years that the director has really come to the fore and taken on the power within the theatre. The modern theatre is a director-led and director-dominated business, even down to the question of fees. It is in the mind of a director that the ideas, decisions and concepts for a production are born. Of course in the 'real' world directors are constrained by budgets and their producers, having to limit their ideas to what can be afforded, even to the extent of how many actors can be employed for a production and who those actors will be.

Planning a production

One of the best ways to prepare for this section of the exam is to go through the process of planning a production of your set texts as if you were the director. Treat it as a real exercise and map out the whole process. As long as your production is justifiable from the text, you should be able to answer whatever question appears in the exam.

Main aim

The overall purpose of a play and its characters is often referred to as the super-objective. As a director you need to decide on the play's main aim and clarify what you want your interpretation to say to the audience. Remember that you cannot offer every single possible interpretation of a play in one production. As we said at the start of this chapter, that is what makes each production of the same play totally different. If you were to put on a production of *A Midsummer Night's Dream* it is highly likely that many in your audience will have seen at least one other production of the play, and most will have some knowledge of what it is about. What is of interest to this kind of audience is what you, as director, have chosen as the play's aim, which themes you have decided to focus on and what you have decided to say to them about the play. It is this decision that will colour all the other decisions you then choose to make, from casting and costume design through to exactly where the actors will stand on stage.

> For more on the super-objective see page 109.

Period

One aspect that needs considering, especially for the earlier plays in this unit, is the period in which you choose to set them. Will your presentation of *Antigone* be historically accurate, or do you feel there is something to be said for setting it in modern dress – maybe into a more recent war zone, or as a commentary on modern tyrannical states? *Antigone* has recently had productions set in Bosnia and in Hitler's Germany, both of which had something specific to say about the chosen periods as well as bringing out the wider issues in the play. Perhaps you could choose a non-specific period, whereby the era is not apparent from the look of the production. This might be successful for *A Midsummer Night's Dream*, for instance, if you wish to create your own world for the play. Or maybe the time period should shift; the scenes in the court could be in one period, say Edwardian England, suggesting a very formal society with clear rules and regulations, and the scenes in the wood could be set in the psychedelic 1960s to suggest a drug-induced dream world. Whatever you choose you must be able to justify your decision.

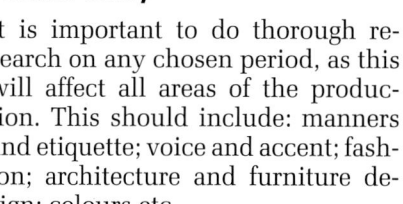

Further study

It is important to do thorough research on any chosen period, as this will affect all areas of the production. This should include: manners and etiquette; voice and accent; fashion; architecture and furniture design; colours etc.

Theatre space

The first technical decision to take is which type of theatre you wish to stage your production in. The choice is wide open to you, but remember that your choice must serve the text and your audience. If you want an intimate experience for your audience in which they are close to the action and the characters, as you might with *The Shadow of a Gunman*, then you would probably not choose to set it in a large proscenium arch theatre or an amphitheatre like the Olivier Theatre. If the play is clearly set indoors then you are unlikely to deliberately choose to direct it as an outdoor promenade in your local park; however, that might be a perfectly valid choice for *A Midsummer Night's Dream*. Do you want a small stage area, or large? This may come down to something as simple as how many actors you need to get on stage at once, but will also reflect the atmosphere you wish to create. Will the play work with an audience on all sides, or should they be watching as if at some distance? Does the play involve journeys from location to location – if so maybe a traverse stage is the answer? See pages 13–19 for some of the different types and layouts of theatres, in order to get some ideas.

Design

Because in the next section of this chapter we will be looking specifically at the designer's approach we will not focus on the design areas of your production here; but remember that as director you do have control of and an input into these areas and can refer to them when writing about your production ideas, as you will see from the suggested essay plans at the end of this section.

Casting

Having chosen your theatre space and made your decisions on the set and other design issues, you are now ready to start work with your actors. However, before you can do that you need to find the right actors for your production through the casting process. Recent past questions have asked you to 'outline your casting ideas for the roles of…' and thus careful consideration must be taken into exactly what is meant by this. As we said in the section on the actor's approach, first impressions make a huge impact on an audience. It is often said that you get or lose a job within the first two minutes of an interview and that will be the same on stage: your audience will decide what they think of a character very quickly. Many professional directors say that 90 per cent of their work is done during the casting process. If you get the right actor for the job then your life as a director is considerably easier. If you get it wrong then the whole process can be a nightmare.

Naturally, much of this is to do with the actor's ability to act, which we can take for granted with your theoretical production, but it is also to do with looks and how the actor sounds. As a director though you must be careful about stereotypes, sometimes it is important to avoid them as it might prevent an audience from learning more about a character and seeing beyond their first impression. Sometimes though you might deliberately choose a stereotype and then subvert this through the way the character is played. If there are some specific physical aspects of a character that are delineated by the text then these must be respected. O'Casey gives some very clear guidelines in *The Shadow of a Gunman* which it would make sense to follow as a director. No one would cast Helena as smaller than Hermia in *A Midsummer Night's Dream*; it just would not work. Nor would you cast them as the same height. In this case part of the casting decision process is done for you, but this is a rare occurrence. With most characters you, as the director, have to make these decisions. Will Demetrius or Lysander be taller for instance, or does it not matter? More difficult are concepts such as age or beauty. How old is old? Clearly Egeus must be old enough to be the father of Hermia, but just how old will you make him? There would be a considerable difference in the way the character is portrayed if you make him 65 or 35, but both are possible and the choice will naturally affect the casting of Hermia. More difficult is the choice of age for Puck, who has often been played as a child, but has also been played as an elderly man. What were those directors saying about the role with such a decision? In *Yerma* you have the difficulty of casting Juan and Victor, one of whom is considered highly desirable by Yerma, the other not. How will you mark this? Do you go for the more stereotyped idea of a strong, manly Victor and a thin, weedy Juan or are you going to be subtler than this and show some individuality? Other aspects to consider when casting include the need to make family

---

Practical exercise

Observe people you don't know, perhaps on a long train journey or walking through the local shopping centre. It is important that they don't notice you observing them. What initial impression do you get from the way they are walking, sitting, moving; the clothes they are wearing; what they are carrying, or maybe reading? Try not to listen in to any conversations as this will give you more than merely visual information.

Think about…

How could you cast Irina, Masha and Olga in *Three Sisters* in order to suggest their relationship. Which aspect of looks will you go for? Facial features, hair length and colouring, height or physicality?

---

relationships believable, nationality and voice. So when discussing your casting ideas refer in detail to the choices you have made and how you would find the appropriate actor to portray them to your audience. Notice how we keep coming back to the audience; they are the important factor.

The next element of direction to consider is the blocking of the play. Blocking is the traffic of actors around the stage. This includes the basic aspects of exits and entrances, how characters get on and off the stage, but more importantly where they go once they are on. The more characters there are on stage at any one time the more difficult this process is. Some directors have this all planned out in minute detail before they start rehearsals, others work more freely and only fix the blocking some way into rehearsals. As a 'virtual' director you really need to work to the former plan, but it is worth experimenting in class on a specific scene to see the effects of different blocking and where the problems lie. Normally, you want to avoid actors 'upstaging' each other. This is where one actor is so much further upstage than the other that the one downstage is stuck with their back to the audience and no doubt very uncomfortable. On the other hand, you might deliberately engineer this effect if you want the character further upstage to have all the focus from the audience. Generally speaking however, you need to consider the positioning of actors relative to each other and the items of furniture or pieces of scenery on stage. Most importantly it is the series of stage pictures that you create that will tell your audience about these characters and their relationships. Remember that in a naturalistic play the moves need to have a motivation; it is very clear when you watch a naturalistic play if the actors have been given moves that have no purpose other than to create stage pictures, their movement will come across as awkward and pointless. It is one of the most common questions from actors to directors – why am I moving over there? To which the answer should not be 'because it looks good'. A better reason will always be to do with character motivation, for example, 'because you instinctively wish to get away from the other character on stage, because you disagree with their point of view'. Remember that you do not have to follow slavishly the stage directions in a text: they may have no relation to your production as your set and stage plan may be very different from the one referred to in the text.

You should now consider how best to reveal the complexity of the relationships between your characters within the scene you are directing. Areas to think about here include: proximity, eye contact, gesture and tactility. In order to look at this in some detail we shall consider the opening scene of *The Shadow of a Gunman* and the developing relationship between Donal Davoren and Minnie Powell. In the play Davoren is a poet and dreamer who has been mistaken by the others who live in the tenement building for a member of the IRA on the run. We are told he has 'upon his body the marks of the struggle for existence and the efforts towards self-expression'. Minnie is described as having an 'easy confidence' and having 'lost the sense of fear… she is at ease in all places and before all persons'. During the course of the scene in which Minnie has pretended to come for a 'drop o' milk for a cup o' tea' but has really

Blocking

Think about…
How would you block the Mechanicals' first scene in *A Midsummer Night's Dream*. Will Bottom be the central focus or will you put Quince centre stage? Where are the others to be placed: around the edges of the stage or all together on one side? What do the different options suggest about their relationships?

Character relationships

come to meet the man she thinks is an exciting and dangerous gunman, the couple gradually come closer and are about to kiss when interrupted by the arrival of another character. As a director working on this scene it will be important to consider the growing proximity between the two and to make clear decisions about how that develops. Davoren is at his writing desk for much of the scene and so it is up to Minnie to make the moves. Will she remain at some distance from him to begin with, or immediately come quite close? This might depend on your interpretation of how much she has 'lost the sense of fear'. Perhaps she will sit on his desk at some point to give her the opportunity of showing her legs, but if so on what line should she do this?

At what precise point will they make eye contact for the first time? This will depend on Davoren mostly; when should he take his eyes off his writing (at the start of the scene he is not interested in being interrupted from his work) and really notice her? When Davoren gives her the milk, will this require him to move or could he just indicate where it is, or is it on his desk and he just holds it out to her? All of these variants will suggest different possibilities for their relationship even at this early stage.

At what moment in the scene will they touch for the first time? When characters first make contact, especially if there is an attraction between them, this can often be a strong moment in the theatre. What is the difference if Minnie touches Davoren or Davoren touches Minnie, and where should they make contact? Does he touch her knee or does she touch his arm? Is it a brief accidental touch, or a lingering, deliberate action? At what point in the scene docs Davoren see the chance he has with this girl and change from disinterested to potential seducer? Is he to be portrayed as a smooth operator or just a chancer? Where exactly are they on stage as he leans in for the kiss? Near one of the beds or standing central? Each one of these choices will affect the overall atmosphere of the scene.

As well as these practicalities, as director you need to consider the pace of the scene and the use of pause. Are there changes in pace or is there a slow build to the climactic moment and the comic timing of the interruption? Will there be any long pauses – perhaps at that moment Davoren realises what is going on – or not?

You can see the minute detail into which the director needs to go while working on a scene. In a real rehearsal the actors will have their own input depending on their own interpretation of the characters, but overall it is the director who must ensure the correct atmosphere has been created for the scene, and therefore final decisions on the physical and vocal work will be yours.

Effects for an audience   Exam questions will often ask you to discuss what specific effects you wish to create for your audience as a director. These are the overall responses that you wish to achieve through your direction of the given scene or scenes. Such effects might be as simple as the creation of laughter, as in the Mechanicals' performance of Pyramus and Thisbe in *A Midsummer Night's Dream*, for example, or more complex, such as gaining sympathy for a particular character or creating a build-up of tension. It might even be along the lines of educating an audience about a particular political situation or current social problem. A production of *Volpone* set in modern dress might be intended to make socio-political comment on our money-hungry society today and the desire to make a quick buck with no regard for moral values.

Sample question 1

Briefly outline your casting ideas for the roles of Antigone and Ismene in *Antigone* and discuss how you would direct the actors in the opening section of the play in order to reveal the characters' relationship to the audience.

Ideas for planning

• Your introduction should state your overall intentions for these characters and how you would wish them to be perceived at the beginning of the play. This is your interpretation of their characters, which you should justify, and then explain how you will show this to your audience through practical performance work.

• Discuss the initial look of both characters – refer to their heights, builds, colourings, costumes and accessories and how they compare to each other. For instance, who is taller, who is older, what colour hair do they have? In order to discuss their costumes you will need to state which period you are setting your production in; but then refer to such elements as shape, colour, cut, length, and general state of clothing. For instance, is Antigone's dress ripped and muddy while Ismene's is clean, perhaps to suggest a symbolism for their decisions, or are they both smartly dressed to show the decision has not yet been made? Is there a colour symbolism you could use for their clothes?

• Discuss their physical and vocal attributes. How do you wish them to sound? Will one have a deeper voice than the other? What accents might they have? Is Antigone showing any sign of stress or is she proud and unbowed? Is Ismene showing any weaknesses in her movement and gesture?

• Work through the scene giving clear and precise direction for some of the major moments in the scene, referring to the use of stage space, distance and closeness between the characters, the use of touch and eye-contact, the use of any items of set you might wish to have on stage. How exactly does Antigone lead Ismene from the palace at the start? How passive will you make Ismene in her refusal to help Antigone, and how aggressive should Antigone be towards Ismene as she tries to persuade her to help? On what specific lines will particular gestures and moves be made? Use quotations from the text at all times to show which sequence of lines you are referring to.

• This should be the main section of your essay and the more detailed you make it the better. Remember that you are trying to make your direction and your interpretation of the relationship between the two characters clear to the reader. They should be able to take your essay and recreate exactly what you have in mind on stage. At all times justify your decisions with reference to the text through the use of quotations.

Remember that staging refers to all aspects of the production and so you will need to refer to set, costume, lighting and sound as well as the movement of the actors around the space.

Sample question 2

How would you stage the opening of Act II of *Three Sisters* and what effects would you wish to achieve for your audience?

Ideas for planning

• You should start by stating what the main effects you wish to achieve for your audience are. Perhaps you wish to indicate the change in the running of the household and particularly the status of Natasha. Equally, you might aim to show the indifference and malaise of Andrey, or to reveal the developing relationship between Masha and Vershinin. Having made your choices these will then be the focus of how you stage the scene.

• An indication is needed of your set and the positioning of furniture in particular and a suggestion for what your choices say about the family background in terms of period and wealth. How will the lighting indicate the evening darkness and the use of candles? Will this mean that certain faces are more in focus than others and how might the actors make use of this? What sound effects are heard from off stage? We are told an accordion is heard faintly in the distance, what is the effect of this? What costumes are the characters wearing? Natasha is in a dressing gown, but what sort? Is it sensible and heavy or thin and flowery? How is Andrey dressed – does his outfit in some way suggest what has happened earlier in the evening? How will you direct the actor playing Ferapont and what will you be saying about him through his costume, voice and physicality?

• How will the various characters move around the set, and how will this show their relationships? Will Natasha and Andrey be seen to be a distance apart throughout, while Masha and Vershinin are close?

• Look directly at specific moments of dialogue and explain how you will stage them. Discuss the pace of the scene and the different characters and what effect this will have on your audience. Are there any moments of comedy to be played upon? Remember that precise detail is always being looked for, along with justification for your ideas based on the text. The essay should be a blueprint for how you want this scene to be staged.

Further reading

Two of the Phaidon Theatre Manuals would be useful: *Lighting and Sound* by Neil Fraser (Phaidon Press 1993) and *Costume and Make-up* by Michael Holt (Phaidon Press 1988).

The designer's approach

The designer's role in any theatre production is to express the director's intentions in a visual manner and, in addition, to solve the practical problems that are presented by the text. The principal task is to create an environment in which the acting can take place, while remembering that whatever decisions are made will also affect the audience's responses to the play – thus they must work in conjunction with the acting and the direction in making statements about the play's themes and actions. When you enter the home of a new friend you usually start to make judgements about their character from the environment in which they live: their choice of colour schemes, furniture, materials, lighting and general housekeeping standards will tell you quite a lot about them. It is the same in the theatre. The audience will judge the characters on the basis of the set design, the choice of lighting effects, the clothes that they are wearing and even the sounds they can hear and thus the role of the designer is vital in helping the audience understand the overall intention of the production. Of course in professional theatre the set, lighting, sound and costume designers are usually all separate people, but for the sake of this exam you have to understand and appreciate the role of each of them and be able to do their work on each of your set texts.

The starting point, as with the director, is the choice of space for the performance. In addition to opting for a particular known theatre set-up, such as a proscenium-arch theatre or in the round, you can always take the decision to invent your own theatrical space for your production. Old factories and workshops, swimming pools and the smallest of rooms above smoky pubs are all viable performance spaces, so don't feel you have to be limited in your choice. The main role of the designer is to create the correct atmosphere for the acting. Therefore it is important that the space is suitable for the play. Think of the difference that takes place when a production moves from the rehearsal room onto the actual set at a dress rehearsal. It is like watching a film without the soundtrack playing in the background and then suddenly hearing the music – the difference is phenomenal. You must also consider the actor/audience relationship. How near will your audience be to the actors and the set, as this will affect exactly what you can do. If the audience is very close you might need a more delicate approach to the scenic painting than if they are at some distance. Their proximity may well affect the levels of lighting required – the closer you are to something the less light you need in order to see it properly. Directional sound effects might work differently if the audience is all around the stage instead of only on one side.

In order to look at the specific requirements of design we will take each of the design roles in turn and see how they would approach a text and the questions they are likely to ask of the director. Work through these questions for your own texts in each case.

Set design

Perhaps the first decision to make is the style of the design, which may or may not be connected to the style of the acting. It is perfectly possible to have completely naturalistic acting on a minimalist set. The style will depend on the main aim you have chosen for your production, but before you can make that decision there are some basic questions to which a set designer needs answers:

How many locations are required by the text and therefore are any changes of set required? If, like *The Shadow of a Gunman*, the whole play takes place in one room then there is less of a problem for the designer than in *Restoration*, where the action takes place in many different locations.

What kinds of locations are there? Does the play take place inside or outside, or a mixture of both? Are all the locations in one environment or are there marked differences? In *Restoration*, for example, there are a vast number of locations in very different

Practical exercise

Put all the various locations within your text at the head of a separate piece of paper. Then add to each the basic requirements as suggested by the text. Think about: the size of the space required; the number of entrances; how many actors use the location; whether there is a need for levels; specific items of furniture required. Then you will be able to add your own ideas for designing this location as you think of them.

environments, including the park, Hilgay Hall, a prison cell, a copse and London Bridge. As a designer for *Restoration*, it will be necessary to find a solution to all these locations that allows for smooth transitions between the scenes while at the same time making it clear to the audience where the action takes place. It may be that simple signs will do, but you may wish to go for a far more complex solution involving revolves, hydraulics or flown scenery. We'll return to the problem of transitions later.

What sort of atmosphere and mood is required by the set design? Is there just one main atmosphere or does this alter through the play? You might say that *The Changeling*'s locations (apart from Scene i), whether in the castle or the madhouse are all fairly similar in atmosphere: dark, oppressive and claustrophobic, whereas in *A Midsummer Night's Dream* there is a vast difference between the court and the wood, and so this will affect decisions about the sort of set you require. High walls and dark colours might suit *The Changeling*, whereas *A Midsummer Night's Dream* might need to be more spacious, airy and colourful.

How many actors are on stage at any one time? You need to know this to determine how much space is required. There is no point having a hugely cluttered and complex setting if there is then no room for the 15 actors who need to appear in Act III. In *Three Sisters*, for example, there are some moments when there are large gatherings of characters, who need space to move. In *Yerma* most of the scenes only involve small numbers of characters, thus less space is required.

How many exits and entrances are required? Even in a non-naturalistic setting you will need to make some arrangements for actors to enter and exit the stage, and there is no point only providing one exit if six are required. In *The Shadow of a Gunman* only one door is required, which leads to the rest of the tenement building, but for the earlier plays the number of entrances to the stage will be entirely at your discretion. By contrast, a farce such as Joe Orton's *What the Butler Saw* is likely to require a lot of doors and split-second timing for rapid entrances and exits.

Are there any levels that are required by the text or which might be helpful in the creation of location? If so, what are they, and how should they connect to stage level? For example, you may feel that in *The Changeling* an upper level is needed to allow De Flores to observe events that are going on, which may require a stone staircase of some kind. Levels and steps will also give the feel of a castle, and can also be used in the madhouse scenes to suggest observation and control of the inmates.

Are there any specific problems to be solved? This, of course, covers a vast range of possibilities, but might include, for example, the river where the washerwomen are working in *Yerma* or Titania's bower in *A Midsummer Night's Dream*. The former will require a decision based on how naturalistic you intend to make the set. Will you have real water flowing across the stage somehow or might you suggest it through the use of a blue cloth? With Titania's bower, you might wish to be able to lower and raise it above the stage through a system of pulleys, or it might be on a

Think about…

How could the use of levels help suggest the status of some characters?

truck that removes it from the stage during the scenes in which she sleeps.

What period is the play being set in? Is this different from the period in which the play was written? This will of course affect all areas of the design.

Look back at the comments made about choosing the appropriate period for your play in the Director's Approach section.

Having got the answers to these questions you can begin to work on the set design and to choose your style. The basic choices are:

Style

Realistic. The set will represent the locations as accurately as possible, so that an audience can believe that the characters are actually in the place stated.

Minimalistic. The set will include only those things that are absolutely necessary. This is the most basic of design styles and often leads to an empty stage. For exam purposes we would not advise you to choose this style if you are going to write about set design, as it will leave you with little to say.

Symbolic. The set will not represent the location, but some aspect of the play. The items on stage or in the background will be directing an audience to a particular interpretation through their understanding of the symbolic nature of the item on stage.

It is possible for set design to encompass a combination of styles, but it is easier to stick to one for the purposes of this examination.

Composite. There will be a structure on set which serves to provide all the different locations required without any change of scenery. This kind of set usually requires lighting effects to bring out smaller areas of the set for each scene.

Expressionistic. The set expresses the themes of the play in a physical form.

Let's take *Yerma* as an example here. A realistic set would clearly represent Andalusian farm cottages and scenery as realistically as possible. This would require research into the area to get a feel for the look of the land. Everything that might be in the cottages would be present on stage in full detail to give a clear impression of the way in which these characters live. For a minimalistic set, there might just be an open stage with a few pieces of simple wooden furniture. You could paint the stage floor to represent the colours of the land and to suggest the dryness and dustiness of the countryside, but there would be little else used. A symbolic set might have objects or images of fertility on stage (such as sheaves of corn to represent harvest and new birth). A composite set would involve no transitions, so there might be one area of the stage used to represent the indoor locations and one area for the outdoor locations, and lighting might be used to show the differences between Yerma's and Dolores' houses. An expressionistic set would suggest a major theme through the way the set is built, so that Yerma's cottage might be built to represent a womb, for example.

You should also consider the size, shape and scale of your design in relation to the actors. Remember, for instance, that if you are creating a naturalistic room there is a difference between a square-edged space and a room full of angles; they will each create a very different atmosphere for your play. The size of items on your set can have a striking affect on an audience. Maybe the bed in *Volpone* should be vast to show how central it is to Volpone's life. The scale of your set

Size, shape, scale

Think about...
How might making the set out of proportion with your actors suggest ideas to your audience about the themes of the play?

is important in reflecting how the characters appear on stage. If your walls tower over the actors then you are suggesting something about oppression and power, for example maybe the palace doors in *Antigone* should be vast to indicate the power of the state.

Materials

You need to choose which materials you will use to build your set. There is a big difference between a structure made of wood and one made of metal. The choice of materials can also reflect the period of the set – a production of *A Midsummer Night's Dream* set in the Elizabethan period should really be constructed of wood, for example. These materials can be disguised and it is the surface that matters here, what the audience assumes the set is made from, not necessarily what it actually is made from. You should have some understanding of the way paint effects can change the nature of the set, and indeed how lighting can also do the same. A good scenic artist can make a stage flat appear to be a heavy, stone wall. There is also the question of reality; are you trying to convince your audience that a tree is real or not? Will your trees in *A Midsummer Night's Dream* be made to look real, or will they be painted to look metallic to give a magical effect?

Further study

If you get the opportunity, visit your local theatre and ask to see their workshop or see some scenery under construction or being painted. This will show you the way simple, cheap materials are completely transformed to look like something else. Materials such as wood, canvas and polystyrene blocks are all used regularly to become something that looks far more expensive on stage.

Colour

Colours are of course vital. As a designer you can say much about the world of your production through the choice of colour. Maybe you will go for drab browns, greys and blacks in *The Shadow of a Gunman* to show the hardships of the time. Will you paint your set for *Yerma* white in order to reflect Andalusian customs, or will there be a more subtle use of colour to reflect some of the themes within the play? Does the period or nationality of the play demand certain colours are used? For example, a Victorian setting might require you to look for the strong reds and greens associated with that era.

Think about…

Consider the symbolism of colour. Why are some colours more restful to the eye while others are more aggressive and unsettling?

Transitions

You must also consider the movement of your set where you have different locations. How will your set function for transitions? Will you use a revolve, which often has some inbuilt symbolism of the world turning or people going on journeys; flown scenery; or maybe trucks (sections of scenery on wheels brought in from the wings)? Even the way in which the scenery changes should serve the needs of the play. Think here about pace especially. You don't want a play like *Restoration*, which has many short scenes, to come to a halt because of the time it takes to change scenes. Find out more about the ways in which locations can be changed on stage, and watch out for how this is done whenever you go and see a production.

Even though you don't have to worry about budget, don't get carried away and have vast trapdoors with hidden hydraulic lifts just to change a piece of furniture.

You may even get a question directly related to how you will create a set to deal with the problem of transitions. If you were asked to explain how you would make the change from the court to the wood in *A Midsummer Night's Dream*, for instance, you might write something along the lines of:

> *The two, ten-foot high stone pillars standing back left and back right will have been built on two revolving platforms which will now revolve slowly to reveal that the backs are painted like two giant tree trunks. A piece of camouflage netting covered with green leaves will be flown in from above to connect with the tops of the trees to give the impression of a vast canopy of foliage above the stage. In the centre of the canopy, flown separately, will be Titania's bower, which will resemble a giant acorn shell. This will be lowered to the floor via a system of pulleys when Titania needs to enter it. The front edge of the shell will be hinged to allow for this. The central truck, on which the two thrones used by Theseus and Hippolyta in the court scene are situated, will be removed on a track to stage right. During the scene change the lights will slowly dim to suggest the coming of evening, and as these changes happen the Fairy and Puck will enter. Puck will be attached to the stage-right tree trunk; there will be hand and foot holds on the trunk, and his costume and the lighting will allow for him to be almost completely camouflaged, so that when he moves it is a surprise for the audience. The fairy will appear via a trap door near the front of the stage. The whole transition will be conducted slowly and to music, and should give the impression of a change from reality to a magical arena.*

Costume design

The use of costume, like environment, can be used in the theatre as yet another way of offering information about the character to the audience. Costumes can also help to locate a play both geographically and historically, and can also suggest the temperature and weather conditions. The way in which a costume is worn can show how comfortable that person is, whether they are relaxed or nervous, whether they are dressing for pleasure or business and whether they are used to wearing the outfit or not. The state of the costume can show both the attitude of the character towards their clothes and also the conditions in which they live.

The questions a costume designer needs to be asking are:

What is the period of the play? This will lead to very detailed research on clothing of that period. It is no good setting the play in the 17th century and then having a few items of costume out of period. There will always be someone in the audience who notices. However, it is also possible to go against period in costume design, but be very careful about why you are doing this, as it must be clear that this is a deliberate effect. Justification, as always, is vital. The Royal Shakespeare Company once contrasted a 'good' brother Edgar, dressed in Victorian frock coat, with a 'bad' brother Edmund, in a sheepskin coat and jingling car keys, in a production of *King Lear* using more than one historical period.

What is the geographical location of the play? This will also affect the style of your design. If the play is set in Spain, then some research about Spanish clothing will be necessary. If you are setting *Yerma* in Andalusia you will need to find out what farmers would be wearing there and not just put them into green Wellington boots and Barbour jackets.

What time of year is the play set in and what is the weather? These answers may not be found in the text, but will be part of the director's decision-making process and therefore should be part of

Further reading

For any late-19th- or 20th-century period, old photographs and magazines are an excellent source for studying costume design. Equally, *Four Hundred Years of Fashion* by Natalie Rothstein (V&A Publications 1999) is an extremely useful book with photographs and drawings based on the collection at the Victoria and Albert Museum. For Elizabethan costume, you'll also find a huge source of information at http://costume.dm.net.

Think about…

What period might you expect to see *The Changeling* or *Volpone* set in? Do they have to be in their original period? Which modern decade might suit each play? Maybe the 1980s for *Volpone*, with its materialism and corporate greed? Maybe the 1920s for *The Changeling*, with its shallow façade of good times and manners covering a multitude of sins?

yours. If the play is being set in a cold climate, then thicker clothes would be worn. In all forms of literature the weather is often used to reflect the mood of the characters. This is called pathetic fallacy. Chekhov uses this device in his plays – the sun is shining hopefully at the start of *Three Sisters*, but by the end of the play the weather is cold and damp to reflect the change in spirit. This needs reflecting in the clothing too, meaning that coats and thicker dresses might be worn in Act IV.

Is the play set indoors or outdoors? Think, for instance, how this might affect the type of shoes the character would wear.

What accessories will be needed? Do the characters need hats or gloves? How much jewellery should be worn? Will the men in *The Changeling* be wearing swords? De Flores needs to be able to conceal a rapier about his person; will he have it hidden under his clothes or perhaps in his boot?

Do the actors have to do any particular moves in the costume? This might restrict what can be chosen, examples being acrobatics (Puck), dancing, fighting.

Will the clothes get wet, or be affected by any special effects? This will affect the material used, silk for instance is not good in the wet, so if using a rain curtain or a mist machine you should not dress your characters in silks.

Having got the answers to these questions, the costume designer (like the set designer) will have further decisions to make.

Style

See the suggested ideas for the appearance of Volpone on page 65 for a particular example of how this can work.

Think about…

Consider the wealth of the characters in your play. Should their clothes look expensive and/or new? In *Restoration*, for example Lord Are is likely to be well-dressed and Bob and Rose are not.

Will the costume design be naturalistic or non-naturalistic? For example, is there to be an exaggerated cartoon look to the design? This might work well for *Volpone* for instance, where costumes might need to be representative of the animals referred to by the character's names. If so, how is this look going to be achieved? Equally, what material or cloth should the costumes be made from? There is a great difference between a dress made of silk and one made of cotton. The choice of material will affect the hang and cut of the clothes. It will depend partly on period, wealth and fashion. It will affect the way an actor moves on stage and might be affected by what an actor has to do in the costume. The choice might also depend on the set design. If there are a large number of awkward stairs or doors, an actress is unlikely to want to have to cope with a long train.

Colour

Are any particular colours required? It may be that specific colours are mentioned in the text. Chekhov is very clear on the colours of the dresses for each of the three sisters, for example. What colour symbolism is required? Colour can also be used to help an audience make associations between characters. So it is often a helpful idea to put characters in the same family within the same colour combinations, or to put characters that are in love in complimentary colours while enemies might clash. It is useful in *A Midsummer Night's Dream* for instance to help your audience by putting Hermia and Lysander in a complementary colour scheme and to do the same for Demetrius and Helena, as often in performance these characters can be confusing if dressed too alike. The opposite idea might work for *Yerma*, where you could put Yerma and Victor into similar colours to show their appropriateness for each other and put Juan into a colour that clashes with Yerma. Bear in mind here that the use of colours should also be thought about in conjunction with set design – you can demonstrate whether a character is at home or out of place in a setting by matching/contrasting their clothing with its colour scheme.

Wear and tear

Should the costumes appear brand new, or should they seem old and worn? Costumes may need deliberately 'breaking down' to achieve the effect of ageing or dirt. Characters should look as if they inhabit their clothes; it is a common mistake of designers to make the clothes seem as if the characters have put them on for the first time that day. Sometimes it is necessary to have two identical costumes, one that looks new and one that is made to look dirty or is covered in blood for example. This saves the problem of cleaning and repairing every night.

Make-up and mask

Plays such as *Volpone*, *Antigone* and *A Midsummer Night's Dream* particularly lend themselves to a consideration of the use of make-up and/or mask. Questions that need to be asked if you are thinking about this include:

> **Further reading**
> *The Complete Make-Up Artist* by Penny Delamar (Thomson 2002) and *Stage Make-Up* by Laura Thudium (Backstage 1999) are useful texts here. Charles Fox Ltd. in Covent Garden, London, conducts some excellent make-up workshops for those interested in this skill.

➤ Will you use half or full masks (remembering that strictly speaking an actor should not vocalise under a full mask)?

➤ What shape and size will the mask be?

➤ Does the mask represent human form or something other than human?

➤ What colours will be used either in the make-up or on the mask?

> **Think about…**
> Masks were worn in Greek theatre to allow the few actors to change character speedily and effectively. It was also a way of representing the gods without offending them as the mask took away all human qualities from the face. The masks were often larger than life to allow the expression to be seen by the audience at the back of the theatre.

➤ Is the make-up meant to be naturalistic, an exaggeration of character (such as making Adolphus Grigson's face in *The Shadow of A Gunman* ruddy with broken veins to suggest his enjoyment of alcohol) or a representation of something else, as with Volpone?

➤ What is the purpose of the make-up – ageing, colouring, to show disease, etc?

➤ What type of make-up will be used – water or grease-based?

Lighting design

The questions a lighting designer needs to be asking are:

Is the lighting to be naturalistic or not? Naturalistic lighting will serve just to light the actors or to create a specific mood irrespective of location.

Where is the location of the scene – indoors or outside? This will affect the intensity and type of lighting looked for. Exterior lighting should be suggested by using lamps to reflect the direction of the sun, with a more natural use of colour: warm yellows for the summer months, oranges and russets for autumn and darker colours to represent winter, for example. Interior lighting should suggest the unnatural tungsten lighting of modern lamps and be placed to show where the interior lighting comes from.

What is the period? It might be that the stage lighting needs to represent lighting by candles, gas or electricity. All will produce a different effect and need different solutions.

Remember that using candles may have implications such as applying for a license: see page 31.

What time of day or night is it? What is the weather? These will clearly affect both the intensity and colour of the lighting. For example, a scene set at dawn should give the suggestion of the rising sun through growing light intensity and the spreading of yellow across the stage. As night falls, the light will change to a bluer, greyer colour and clearly dim in intensity. Stormy weather would require a darker light. Clouds can be created with the use of moving gobos.

What direction will the lighting come from? For an outdoors scene a lighting designer will want to know the location of the sun; for one indoors, where the supposed light sources are. The effect of this is to create a sense of truth. In addition it might be that you want to use creative lighting for special effect, such as the use of upward lighting to create vast shadows on the cyclorama, or to light a face from underneath to create some tension or horror – it is very unnatural to see someone lit from below, which is why the use of torches on stage can be so effective. This sort of lighting could be very effective in *The Changeling* for instance. In the scenes that lead to the murder of Alonzo, both characters could be carrying flaming torches (depending on the health and safety aspects of your chosen set), which would create a flickering effect on their faces and would need limited additional lighting from the rig.

What is the intensity of the light? Should the scene be dimly lit or bright?

What colours are required? Colour in lighting is provided by placing a gel in front of the lamp. The most obvious uses are blue to create the effect of night time, greens to give a feeling of trees and countryside, and reds to symbolise danger and blood.

Are any gobos required? A gobo is a stencil placed in front of a lamp in order to project a shape onto the stage. These can vary from the break-up effects like leaf patterns etc. to signs and images (the Eiffel tower to suggest that we are in France, for example).

What mood is being looked for at each lighting change? What is the pace of the fade from one state to the next? A quick fade will have a very different effect from a slow fade.

Sound design

Sound design covers any sounds that are created to enhance the atmosphere of the production. It includes the use of music to create mood as an underscoring as well as all natural sounds. Things to consider when thinking about sound are:

Is the music to be played live or pre-recorded? Live music might be played on stage or in the pit, as one might find at a musical for instance. It could also be that the musicians are there as characters within the play. For example, for the Bergomask at the end of the performance of 'Pyramus and Thisbe' in *A Midsummer Night's Dream* you might choose to bring a small group of musicians on stage as members of the community, or just have music playing as if from offstage through the speakers.

Further study

If you are going to write about lighting design in any great detail you should understand the different types of lamps available and the sort of light they produce. Floods, fresnels, profiles and birdies are all different examples and are used for different effects (see page 18). Find out too about the use of shutters to control the shape of a beam of light from a lantern.

A good lighting designer will have a vast range of gels for every different occasion.

Web link

There are a number of useful images illustrating the effects of different types of lighting at http://dolphin.upenn.edu/~pacshop/examples/rad-examples.html

Is the music 'real' or underscored? Do the characters on stage hear the music or is it as in a film, i.e. the audience can hear the music but the characters can't.

How real should the sound be? It might be that the sound required is more symbolic than natural. For example it might be decided that when Oberon squeezes the love potion into Titania's eyes there should be a sound effect that goes along with it to imply the magic taking place; a clear decision will need to be taken on exactly what this sound is.

The technical terms for 'real' and 'underscored' are 'diegetic' and 'non-diegetic'.

What direction should the sound come from? Should it be heard through all the auditorium speakers, or should it come just from one direction? For instance the sound of a dog barking, which the characters refer to, should probably just come from the direction in which the dog is meant to be.

What is the intensity of the sound? With real off-stage sounds, such as a dog barking, this might depend on the distance the source of the sound is meant to be from the stage. With music it will depend on the actors' voices and the required atmosphere.

Sound design can also be used to enhance or alter the actors' voices. You might wish them to sound as if they are in a vast empty cavern and thus add an echo effect. Or an actor playing a ghost might need some effect added to their voice. This can be achieved through the use of microphones and distortion.

Other technical effects

Part of the overall design will be the use of technical effects that, strictly speaking, do not fall into any of the categories above, but often come under the auspices of the lighting department. Areas to consider here include:

Projection of slides or video work. This is often done via Microsoft PowerPoint presentations and the use of computer graphics. This might simply be to give scene titles or locations of scenes on the cyclorama, or might be used to show video images of events happening elsewhere in the play. For *The Shadow of a Gunman* for example it might be helpful to have video images of the Easter Rising or other important historical events playing either before or during the play on a video screen.

Pyrotechnics. These are explosive devices used on stage for dramatic effect. Useful perhaps in *A Midsummer Night's Dream*.

Smoke, mist or snow machines. These are used to represent either the reality of smoke, mist or snow, or to create atmosphere. They combine extremely well with lighting to create a powerful effect on stage.

Rain curtain. This is a device that allows water to fall on stage, which requires quite a complex system of pipes and drainage. Although it falls only in one strip across the stage (as in a curtain) through lighting it can look as if rain is falling on the whole stage. Naturally this has quite an effect on the actors and the costumes.

Remember that when answering a question the quickest way of imparting some design information is through sketches. You should make use of them, but ensure that they are fully labelled. For set design the overhead plan or front view work best, but be careful not to mix the two. Always indicate where the audience is located. Costume designs should be thoroughly labelled to give indications of the materials, colours and state of the clothing. It is perfectly ac-

Use of sketches

For an example of an actual student's use of a sketch to convey design information, see the picture of 'Victor' on page 88.

ceptable to use coloured pens or pencils when working on sketches in the exam. Remember though that they are sketches not pieces of art – as long as they are clear it will not matter if you are not the greatest artist in the world, and you really don't have time in the exam room to be one.

Sample question

As a designer, how might you use colour in your setting, lighting and costume designs in order to create the appropriate mood and atmosphere for Act II Scene i in *Yerma*?

Ideas for planning

• Your opening statements should give your overall interpretation of this scene in terms of mood and atmosphere. This might be to create a sense of ritual, to suggest the claustrophobic nature of the rural community, to show the isolation of Yerma from this community or a combination of these (or something else entirely).

• Referring to Lorca's own stage directions at the top of the scene, give an indication of how you will create the sense of a fast-flowing mountain stream: will it be real water, suggestive cloth or some other device for creating the stream? What colours will you use? The areas to think about here are the rocks, the river itself and the general surface of the ground around the stream. What will the colour used to show the river suggest – will it be a pure blue to suggest purity and clarity, or a murkier colour to suggest a lack of cleanliness? Is there to be anything growing near your river? Any greenery to suggest fertility and new birth? If so, will Yerma's sisters-in-law be standing in a brown, barren area of ground to represent Yerma's isolation from the others?

• In terms of lighting design, will you go for a strong yellow to represent the heat of the countryside, with maybe some use of orange? Is the strength of the sun to be represented coming from one direction through colour? Are you going to use colour to suggest the time of day? Will you enhance the idea of the stream by using some blues in your lighting? Perhaps you feel there should be a change in the intensity of light and use of colour on the sisters-in-law's entrance; perhaps there is a sense of clouds covering the sun so that the scene becomes greyer and less yellow? How will colour be used in conjunction with intensity and direction of light? Will you make use of any gobos or special effects to affect the mood and atmosphere?

• In costume design will you dress the washerwomen in a series of bright colours to highlight their joyful nature; or are they all in one colour to represent their uniformity in society? Will you want to distinguish some of the women more than the others through colour? The first woman for instance seems to take a different attitude. What colour will the clothes that they are washing be? The sisters-in-law are described as wearing black in the stage directions; will you therefore make a focus of this through the choice of materials? (A heavy material will seem blacker than light cotton, for example, and this will also depend on the lighting used on them.)

• Although the focus of the question is on colour and the creation of mood and atmosphere, it is relevant to bring in other aspects of the design that help to enhance the mood in combination with colour.

• Finish by referring again to your intentions as a designer in relation to the use of colour and how you have combined its use within your setting, lighting and costume choices to create a particular mood and atmosphere.

 Test yourself

1. As a director, how would you present the chorus in their opening section and the confrontation with Creon in *Antigone*, and what effects would you wish to achieve for your audience?

2. As a designer, discuss your ideas for the use of costume and setting design in Act V of *A Midsummer Night's Dream* in order to create comedy for your audience.

3. As a designer, how would your setting ideas for Volpone's bedchamber reflect the themes you would wish to establish for your audience?

4. How would you perform the role of Alsemero in *The Changeling* in Act I Scene i in order to establish your interpretation of the character for your audience?

5. How would you perform the role of Seamus in Act II of *The Shadow of a Gunman* and what effects would you wish to achieve for your audience?

6. How would you want the audience to respond to Bob in Part One, Scenes iv and v in *Restoration*, and how would you perform the role in order to achieve your aims?

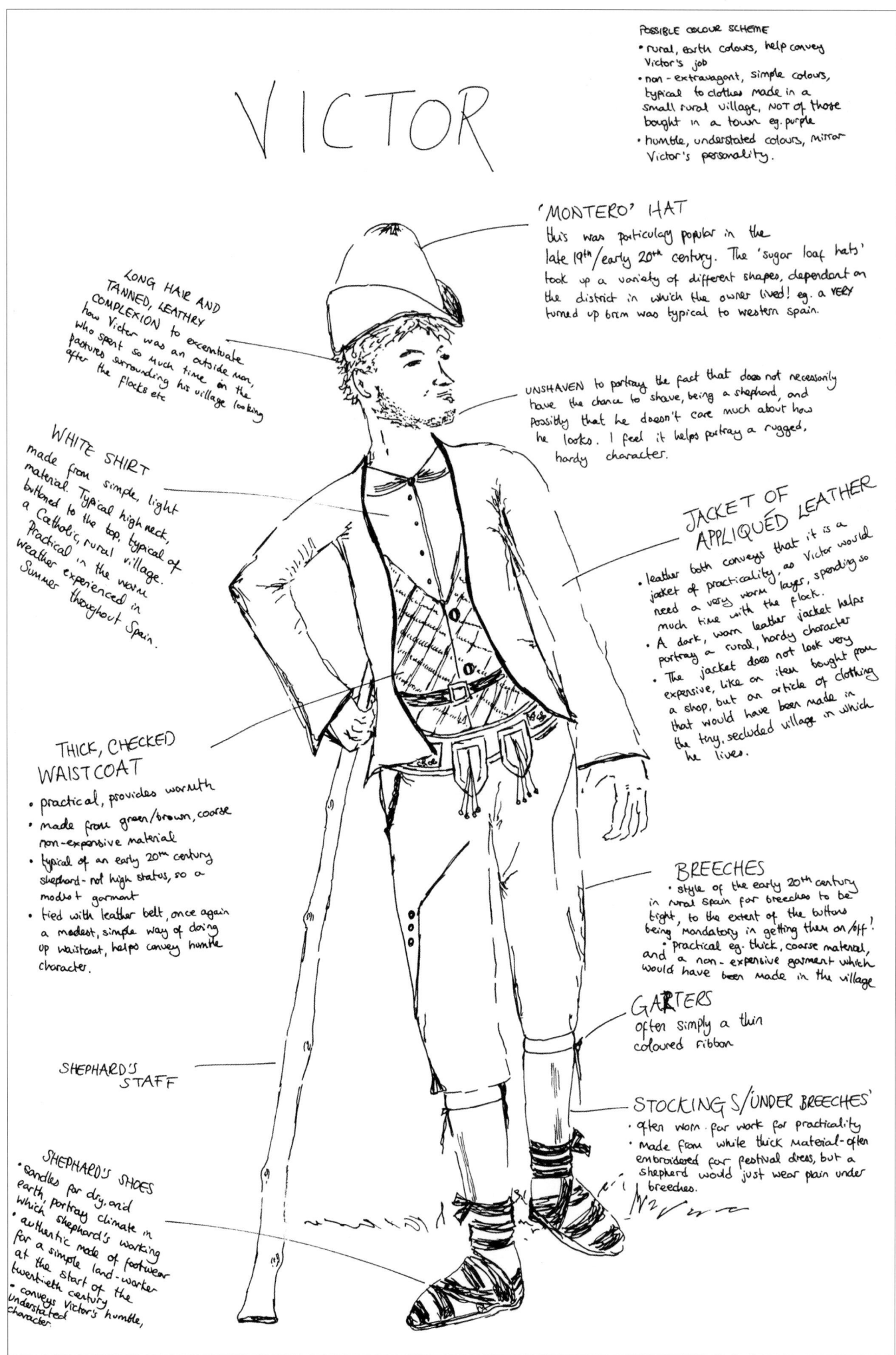

Theatre in Practice – Response to Live Theatre

In this section we aim to give you a method for responding to the live theatre productions that you will see during your course. The questions in the exam will ask you to give a personal, detailed evaluation of an aspect of a production, whether it is related to an element of the acting, design or directing, or is a response to a more general aspect, such as how the production made you react as an audience member.

Because the emphasis is on analysis and evaluation rather than memory, you are allowed to take notes on the productions you have seen into the exam room. For **each** production you are allowed to write a maximum of **two** sides of A4. You may take in notes for as many different productions as you wish: we would recommend at least two, and no more than four. These notes will be collected in with your exam script and sent to the examiner, who will have access to them when marking your paper. It is very important to structure your notes carefully and usefully – we shall look at ways to do this later in the chapter.

It is important also to remember that for this section of the exam you CANNOT write about productions of any of the plays that constitute set texts for AS or A2, although you may well have chosen to see them to help with the study of your texts.

Much of what we discuss here will refer back to the chapter on Approaches to Text, as in essence you will be working in a similar way. The director, actors and designers will have gone through that process while working on the production, and so your job now is to see if you can work out what answers they came up with and to decide how successful they have been in transferring that text to the stage.

Before the performance

What sort of productions should you see? The answer is that any live theatrical production will give you food for comment. It does not have to be a professional piece of work; amateur performances are equally acceptable. Nor does it have to be a piece of straightforward drama either: musicals, physical theatre work, circus, street theatre, dance and opera can all be valid, although pop music concerts, however attractive, are not suitable. In fact, the greater variety of theatre you see the more you will learn about the nature of live performance and how productions are put together, which is the point of this section of the course. Try to ensure you have seen both humorous and serious productions if you can. The production does not have to be successful or one which you thought was outstanding – a poor performance can give many opportunities for critical writing, as long as you can analyse why it was poor. The

Notes

Set texts

Set texts

Section A: The Greeks to the Jacobeans:
- Sophocles – *Antigone*
- Shakespeare – *A Midsummer Night's Dream*
- Jonson – *Volpone*
- Middleton – *The Changeling*

Section B: The 20th Century and Contemporary Drama
- Chekhov – *Three Sisters*
- O'Casey – *The Shadow of a Gunman*
- Lorca – *Yerma*
- Bond – *Restoration*

most important attitude that needs to come through in your response is an enthusiasm for and enjoyment of theatre, whether you are praising or being highly critical of what you have seen.

Preparation

Sometimes it is not possible to do any preparation before going to see a production. If, for example, you are going to see a new play by a new writer there might be very little information available on either the piece or the playwright. The same is often true of physical theatre work, though there might be information on the company performing which could be useful. There is also a great delight to be had from going to see something about which you have no prior information, so that you enter the theatre with absolutely no idea of what you are going to see. You will have no expectations, and therefore will respond instinctively to what you witness and should enjoy attempting to analyse later why the piece made you respond in the way you did.

Expectations

However, it is also important on occasions to do some work prior to attending the performance. For the sake of this exam we would advise you to see **at least** one production of a play you have read or researched before you go. This is so that you can discuss the interpretation with some sense of clarity. In addition you will be able to refer to how the production did or did not fulfil your expectations. So if it is a performance of a well-known play (a Shakespeare text, for example), read the script before you go and get some ideas in your mind of how you would expect the piece to be performed. This should include thoughts on staging as well as interpretation of character and theme. What are you expecting your emotional response to be? Are you expecting to laugh or be moved by the performance? Look back at page 51 where you were asked to respond initially to your set texts and follow the same sort of pattern with the play you are due to see.

Research

It may be that you can conduct some research on the company which is performing. This will give you some ideas regarding how they approach their work. Anyone attending a production by Théâtre de Complicité, for example, would be expecting a very physical production where the performers will use their bodies and simple props to suggest different effects. Try to find websites about the company, director, playwright and venue before you go.

It is often possible to read newspaper reviews of a production you are going to see. Although this is a valid exercise and can help you to think about your expectations, it can also be dangerous in that you may assume that the reviewer is correct. Remember that a newspaper critic is only writing their opinion and it may be that you will totally disagree with them once you have seen the production. If you are going to look at reviews, then look at a number of them to see if there is a general agreement or a huge difference of opinion concerning the piece. But, either way, when you go to the production be open to it and ensure that you form your own opinion.

As an overall structure for a critical response to live theatre we suggest the following four steps: **watch**, **describe**, **analyse**, **assess**. Let's look at these in turn.

Watching the production

Do **NOT** make notes during the production. There is nothing worse than seeing an auditorium full of students with notepads on their knees, frantically scribbling throughout the performance. It is highly irritating to other audience members and actors loathe it. Not only is it distracting for everyone else, but it also means that you are not watching the performance in front of you; your focus is on your notepad rather than on the stage. There are some wonderful stories of actors stopping productions in mid-flow to tell members of the audience to put their notebooks away, and we would certainly have sympathy with them.

However, it is fair to say that you will not be watching the play in the same way that a member of the general public will be. Of course you should follow the story and react to the performance on an emotional level, but you must also watch with a trained eye. How is the production being put together? Look up at the lighting rig for instance to see what sort of lamps are being used and how the lighting effects are being created. Notice the costumes and look for the small details of accessories. Be aware of the way the actors are moving and creating their characters through gestures and vocal work. Have a good look at the set and the way any changes are made. You will be making notes on all these aspects later, and probably be discussing them in class, so it is important to observe them carefully during the production.

Notes

Observation

Describing the production

The ability to describe aspects of the production clearly and concisely is vital. Always remember that you will be writing for someone who has not seen the production you have. Even if you are writing about *Blood Brothers*, which the examiner might well have seen, it is unlikely that they saw the same performance as you on the same night and thus there will be differences. Therefore it is important that you are able to make your examiner see in their mind's eye the same thing that you saw on stage, and you will only be able to do this through your powers of description.

 Try this simple exercise to help you work on the skill of description.

Shortly after watching a production (this really ought to be no later than the next day) choose one moment of the performance that left a strong impression on you and try to write a complete description of exactly what happened on stage during that moment. The chosen moment should only last a few minutes at most, but ideally will encompass both performance and production elements. Your piece of description should be one paragraph only. Having written your piece, show it to someone who was not at the production. If they are able to picture that moment from what you have written then you have been successful. If not, ask them to point out which parts of your description are unclear and work on those sections until they are happy.

For example, with reference to a recent National Theatre production of *Jumpers* by Tom Stoppard, you might start by writing:

> At this point in the play Dotty was trying to prevent the Inspector from seeing the body of the acrobat that she had hidden in her cupboard. We already knew that the Inspector had a crush on her, as she was a famous actress, and thus had no suspicions of her anyway. As he entered her room she was standing on the bed, wearing a long silk shirt only and posing as if for a photograph. At this point the other door blew open and a strong wind came through which made her hair and shirt swirl around her. The Inspector stood stock still with his mouth open and was clearly awe-struck.

Although this passage gives some indication of what happened there are only a few details and it is unlikely that someone who had not seen the performance has a clear image of the scene. There is no mention of set, colours, lighting, sound, acting skills and so on. We have no idea what this room looked like, for instance, and certainly no real impression of why the scene had such an impact. So you could build it up in the following way:

> At this point in the play Dotty was trying to prevent the Inspector from seeing the body of the acrobat that she had hidden in her cupboard. We already knew that the Inspector had a crush on her, as she was a famous actress, and thus had no suspicions of her anyway, but there was a building of tension as to whether she would manage to hide the body in time. This was deflated by the hugely comic moment as he entered her room, provided by a combination of many production elements. Dotty's bedroom was like a boudoir; the bed was heart-shaped and covered in a thick white fur throw. Around her bed hung white curtains on a track. Having hidden the body, the actress leapt onto the bed and closed the curtains round her. The bedroom was on a large revolve and as the Inspector stood on stage right the bedroom revolved to meet him. At the moment he stepped onto the revolve a pair of double doors far stage left swung open. A wind machine offstage came on combined with a strong bright light from the same direction, so that as Dotty threw back the curtains they billowed around her and she was bathed in a powerful white light. She was now dressed only in a long pale blue silk shirt that also billowed up revealing her long perfect legs. She was creating the iconic pose of Marilyn Monroe for the Inspector who stood as if thunder-struck at this awesome image. The speed with which all this happened was so quick and effective that the audience responded with huge laughter and applause. I found it a highly successful moment of theatre.

This now gives a far stronger picture of the scene and also incorporates a personal response suggesting why it was a powerful moment in the production.

Another exercise to try is to describe in full detail the set from a production you have seen. Again be aware that you are writing for someone who has not seen this set and so be their eyes for them. The best way to do this is to start from one side of the stage and work your way round; ideally from stage right to stage left as this is the way we tend to look at things. Remember to give every detail and to describe each item in turn. Think about such things as size, shape, scale, texture and colour.

For example, again referring to *Jumpers*, George's desk was positioned far stage right. To say 'there was a desk there' is not enough. Try:

> It was a large, rectangular, antique wooden desk, which had drawers on either side. The top was completely covered in papers, boxes, books and general clutter, so that it looked as if the owner lived in a total mess. All around the desk was further clutter. The chair was a wooden office-type chair on wheels; the seat and arms were made of studded brown leather, which looked worn and slightly frayed at the edges.

The more detail you are able to give, the more you are able to analyse the reasons why the design is the way it is. Of course if you are writing about set design then it is helpful to draw a sketch of the set layout or sections of it. Refer to the section on use of sketches on page 85.

Analysing the production

Having worked on your ability to describe what you have seen you need to be able to analyse the production. You will be expected to use theatrical terminology correctly and with ease when analysing a production, as with all the written sections of this exam. It is important therefore that you understand the meaning of the words in the Understanding Theatre chapter and are able to use them correctly in context. However, you should not feel that you must use a formal approach when writing a production essay. The most important thing that must come across to the examiner is your enthusiasm for and appreciation of the live theatre that you have seen – don't forget that you can still be quite critical in an enthusiastic manner. If you are able to explain why you think a production failed, while showing an understanding of how the production was put together and what elements of it did or did not work, then you will interest the examiner as much as if you are being hugely positive about the whole experience.

The main question you need to ask yourself is what was the production trying to achieve and how did it go about doing this? In order to answer this question you need to work through all the following aspects and elements of the production in some detail. If you make detailed notes as you go you will later be able to hone these down to the notes you will take into the exam room.

Directorial interpretation

It is very important to have some understanding of what the director's interpretation of the text is. If you have read the play before-hand, or done some research into the piece then you should be able to appreciate which themes or ideas are being presented by this

Further study

Try writing to the director of a production that particularly impressed you, asking what they felt was the most important aspect of their interpretation, and how they tried to bring that out for the audience.

production. The theme should come across in the staging and set design – the way certain characters and relationships are focused upon, even the choice of colour schemes in the costumes will suggest certain ideas. It may be that, in order to show the director's viewpoint, certain characters are presented more or less sympathetically than you might have expected. Look closely at the way characters are positioned on stage – most directors will allow the focus to be on the characters that support their interpretation by placing them in a central or strong upstage position. For example, if directing *King Lear*, one director might place Lear himself centre stage in the opening scene to allow the audience to look at his character and see how he feels about his daughters, whereas another director might place him downstage with his back to the audience to allow the focus to be on the daughters, so that we watch their decision process and see how they feel about their father.

In the opening scene of *King Lear*, an aged king forces his three daughters to state how much they love him in order to decide how much of his kingdom they should inherit.

Programme

Where you know nothing about the play you are about to see, a good source of information can be the programme. It is always worth buying one, not just so that you can assign the various characters their real names (though this is important – if purely to be able to make a clear distinction between actor and character), but also for the programme notes which will often give you clues about the production's aims and the director's interpretation. After the performance make a note of those ideas in the programme that you felt were brought out by the production and those that were not.

If you get the chance to talk to the director or the actors before or after the performance it is always fascinating to see how their ideas took shape through the rehearsal process. It is surprising how often the really important and striking ideas that underpin a whole production come unexpectedly during the rehearsal period and were not necessarily thought out beforehand.

You could try encouraging your teacher to take you to productions that have talks, workshops and masterclasses attached to them.

Choice of staging form

Is the choice of staging form appropriate for the production? Remember that the theatre building itself is part of the staging form. If you saw a two-hander play that was touring the country, you may have seen it in a large, Victorian building and felt it was dwarfed by such a vast space and was therefore lacking intimacy, which you might have felt was important for the play. Or the reverse could be true – a large, epic play might have felt constricted if performed in a small modern studio theatre. Is the space a formal or informal space and how does that affect the production and your response to it? Although we don't want you to write about your experience of getting to the theatre (no discussion of bus journeys and whom you were sitting next to required!) the distance of your seat from the stage, or angle of view could be important when discussing your opinion of the production, so do think about this aspect.

Think about...

Would a comedy sit better in an end-on theatre or in-the-round? What is the effect on an audience of a theatre that uses house tabs (a curtain in front of the stage)?

Stage setting and design

Having worked on your own set designs for your set texts, you should have an understanding of the way set design enhances a production. When commenting upon someone else's designs you should think about how they supported the production: what did they add to the understanding of the world in which the characters of the play live? Think about the use of colours and materials. Was the design naturalistic, symbolic or expressionistic? If you work though the series of questions asked on pages 77–79 and consider how the designer may answer them, then you will be able to comment fully on the set design, and should be able to analyse why those choices were made and what the designer was trying to say to the audience through them.

Further study
With a production that you have seen, consider what other stage settings might have been used. Try to come up with a stage plan that is completely different from the one that you saw. How would it alter the interpretation of the play?

Use of space

Think about the way the production used the space available to it. Did the design fill the space and make it convincingly become somewhere else? How many areas were used on stage – was it all one space or was it divided by set or lighting into a number of different areas through the production? How did the actors use the space? Did they seem comfortable within it and use it appropriately, or did you feel that they hadn't really connected with the space they were working in? How many levels were used during the production and how effectively were they used?

Think about...
In what ways might a production use the auditorium space? What is the effect on an audience when actors come among them rather than staying separate from them on the stage?

Creation of pace

It is very often the pace of a production that can make or break it. If the pace is too slow then the audience is likely to become bored or simply not care about the action taking place. On the other hand if it is too quick then the audience may feel they are not being given time to become involved in or to respond to the play. A good director will find ways to change the pace through a number of methods to ensure that the audience is kept on its toes and interested in what they are watching. Was there a variety in the pace – did the pace build up to climaxes within the play, or was there a continuously steady pace throughout? Pace can be affected by many elements within the production so look out for the following. Did the actors speak their lines clearly, with good diction and at a pace that ensured you could always understand what they were saying? Were there any pauses that seemed too long? This includes the transitions between scenes as well as during them: a good performance can easily be destroyed by long scene changes. What was the pace of the lighting changes – smooth or sharp? Was the pace appropriate for the style of the play?

Think about...
In what ways and why might a farce have a different pace from a more serious piece?

Performance skills

You need to be able to analyse the performers' skills. These range from how the actors portray character through voice and movement to their use of specialist skills such as singing, dancing, acrobatics and so on. Again, look back at the section on the actor's approach to text on pages 62–68 to explore the ways in which an actor may produce a character. Think about how the actors within the production you are analysing did this. You should think about the usual elements of voice (volume, pitch, pace, pause, accent) and the elements of movement (gesture, stance, walk and facial expressions). How effective was each of the actors in these areas and what do you feel they did to establish their character? Did they integrate their use of movement and language appropriately? How

For an example of a high-grade exam answer on this topic, see pages 9–12.

Think about...
Was the casting appropriate? Did the actors suit their roles physically?

did they use props and accessories to help in their portrayal of character? Was their singing/dancing of good quality? Had they the appropriate acrobatic/clowning/mime skills required for the role? Most importantly, were they convincing in what they did?

Costume

What did the costume design say about the characters in the play and its setting? Refer to pages 81–83 to understand the way a costume designer approaches a text and, by examining those questions, see if you can decide what the costume designer of this production was trying to tell the audience about the characters and the world of the play. How were colours and materials used to inform you about the status and relationships of the characters? Think also about hairstyles and accessories. Was there a particular period that had to be conveyed to the audience? How was this done? How did the actors wear their costumes, did they look comfortable in them? Did the costumes affect their movement?

Lighting and sound

Analyse the way the technical elements enhanced the production. Was the lighting used merely to define space, or was it suggesting something more through the use of colour and the creation of mood and atmosphere? What sort of lamps were used and what was the effect of this? Were any gobos or gels used and how effective were they? What was the pace of the lighting, were there any sudden surprises or was it all very subtle?

How was sound used? Were the effects all real or were they used to enhance mood? Did the production make use of music (either live or recorded) and to what end? What direction did the sound effects come from? Was there any use of projection or special effects such as smoke or rain machines? One of the most important things to consider here is whether the technical elements were a necessary part of the production or did they seem to be there merely for the sake of it?

Actor/audience relationship

Often one of the hardest things to analyse is why the relationship between the actors and the audience either worked or did not work. It may be that you were sitting in the auditorium completely turned off by the production while all around you people seemed to be thoroughly enjoying themselves. It may be that you were simply not in the right mood for the play that day and no matter how good the performance was it could not reach you. However, there are times when the whole audience seems uninspired by a production and that is likely to be down to the relationship between the actors and the audience. Even in a totally realistic performance the actors need to be able to make contact with their audience. This can come down to energy. Are the actors really working, do they seem to have faith in the success of their product? If the performers are making little effort then the audience will remain cold. The space can also affect this and the positioning of the performance in relation to the audience. As a member of the audience you need to be able to assess all this and reflect upon it.

?

Think about…

Consider the ways that a costume designer collaborates with a set designer. What are the different points being made if the set and costume colours complement or clash with each other? What effect does lighting have on costumes? How do the different costumes work together and with the other elements within the production as a whole?

?

Think about…

In what way is sound used to promote a particular reaction from an audience? Consider how you would create the sound effect of approaching footsteps in the audience to make your audience laugh, or be afraid.

?

Think about…

How do actors make the audience listen and be interested in what they have to say? Why is it that some voices are more appealing to our ears than others?

Assessing the production

The final part of the process is your personal assessment of the success or failure of the production. After you have analysed and have given a detailed examination of all the elements of the performance you must give your own evaluation. Were your expectations on entering the auditorium realised or not? Did the production achieve its aims, as you perceived them? Only you can answer this question and there are no right or wrong answers here. As long as you have been able to support your opinion through your detailed analysis then your opinion is totally valid. It is a form of constructive criticism that is looked for. Always qualify your views with reference to what took place on the stage and don't generalise or be vague.

Notes

You are allowed to take up to two sides of A4 notes for **each** production into the exam with you. These notes must not include programmes, scripts or any printed articles. They must be entirely written by you.

It is advisable to write your notes on a computer so that you can edit them easily as you work on them and, of course, you can write more this way than by doing them by hand (though beware of cramming in as many words as possible in size 8 font – you need to be able to read them easily!). Make sure your notes are clearly in note form. Whole paragraphs that you could copy out in the exam are not allowed. We would suggest you use headings and bullet points as your format. It might help as a starting point to use the sections above as your headings.

Decide which elements of each production you want to write on in the exam and only write notes that are relevant to those elements for that production. If you are using one production for a possible essay on acting, then focus on that in your notes; do not have copious notes about the sound and lighting. Likewise if you saw a play which had a fascinating set design then write the bulk of your notes on that aspect rather than the acting. However, you should make sure that one of your productions is suitable for an essay on the overall production (and its directorial interpretation) and thus your notes for that one will be on all aspects.

Always remember that your notes will be sent with your script to the examiner. If you are unsure about the validity of any aspect of your notes check with your teacher before taking them into the exam.

Here are two sides of student notes on a play called *Creaking Shadows*, inspired by the short stories of Edgar Allan Poe. Obviously, you may not have seen this play or wish to write on it, but this should give you an idea of how to structure your own notes for the exam.

Creaking Shadows
Trading Faces Theatre Co
Stahl Theatre
November 2003

➤ **Genre** – ghost story. Physical theatre with masks, comic elements and modern dance.

➤ **Director's interpretation** – to entertain, to scare (enjoyable and fun).
Audience response good = successful. Insight into Edgar Allen Poe's life – used references to his stories – picture, book, poem. References to his segregation from family, need to belong. Need for relationships shown by ghost (hugs Emily's leg). Did not need to know about Poe to enjoy play.
Gothic horror theme – darkness, creaks, haunted old mansion, death, murder, mystery left unexplained, ghost, psychological element.

➤ **Audience's response** – screams, jumps, laughter often after screams, expectation of reaction e.g. cowering, so tension created. Did not overdo scary moments, tension built up well, audience remained focused, kept a fine line – audience could have lost interest but only 1hr 10 mins, no interval, kept atmosphere. Age limit (over 13) so focus is kept. Sadness when grandma dying = intense.

➤ **Performers' skills** – dance (not man, but had to move with rhythm, mask work, movement, voice, quick costume changes (back stage) to create confusion and scares.
Mask = half mask for three characters, full mask for ghost. Ghost-mask looked serious and scary. Walked slowly as though had heavy feet, stood upright.
Dennis – most naturalistic. Not much physical movement, moved faster, slight hunch, clear two different characters. Voice – changed, with Emily either loving or complaining about wanting to leave, around Nana louder, sarcastic. Often hugged Emily.

Emily – worried expression with raised eyebrows on mask connected into hair – neat, light brown bob. 30 from clothes – knee length brown skirt with matching jacket for opening scene only, then red silk trousers and shirt. Moved in flustered panicky way, short steps, constant movement. In dance sequence – fluid, flowing, continuous, ballet. Voice – high pitched, fast pace, stuttered at times, serious tone, slightly nervous. Often glanced at audience showing full-face front, sharing emotions with audience, freeze-frame image of emotion. With change of angle of light expression slightly changes, ghosts glowed. Never touched face.

Nana – mask had glasses, brought focus to eyes, made more realistic, less mask-like, brought out naturalistic acting. Real surprise at end when mask off – actor about 22! Expected much older so good performance skills. Movement – walked slow, favoured left leg, hobbled, short steps, curved back, put hand on back sometimes showing pain, slippers caused shuffling. Naturalistic though slightly exaggerated. Early 70s. Mask was smooth so didn't bring age. When became Emily's double moved very well and easily. Mimicked Emily a few seconds afterwards, gave staggered strange effect like on drugs, as she'd been given drug overdose by ghost.

- ➢ **Set design** – dark colours, deep browns and blacks, typical of pensioner emphasising age of Nana, and age difference between Nana and the other two characters.

  Location – big creepy house in remote area. Felt isolated.

  End on open stage, lighting gave impression was bigger than was by suggesting kitchen, stairs, hall (lights off stage but could be seen through exit) and sound effects (front door opening etc). Tall ceilings gave impression big house.

  Levels – stairs and ground. Gauze separated them – used to create surprise appearances of ghost.

  Period – modern day.

  Wallpaper faded.

  Bright orange sofa = big contrast to rest. Nana wore similar coloured dressing gown and gave one to Emily, showing ownership of space and segregation of Dennis.

  Style = old fashioned, Victorian, looked a little creepy as dark, hanging chandelier, creepy atmosphere.

  Practicality – string attached to cat food tin (actor had to watch out), 2 entrances from stairs (stage right) and entrance stage left. Coffin had a hole upstage which actress (Nana) could roll out of to change costume and character.

  No movement of set apart from props, no set changes.

  Overall design effect on audience – dark, mysterious, enhanced style of play. High ceiling = big house, flickering light = creepy, swinging light represented time passing and confusion. Gauze gave mystery as ghost could suddenly appear = shock. Could not see actor behind gauze without light there. Mysterious and scary feel for upstairs. Picture of Poe focal point, always there, constant reminder, echoed theme of play – on gauze – face appeared at end through this.

  Impact – brought scary and gloomy atmosphere. Gauze enabled frights.

- ➢ **Lighting** – gave shocks as would suddenly make ghost appear and controlled where the audience looked. Generally quite dark – bringing sinister atmosphere, especially when light was off stage. Showed what time of day it was. Blue gels for night.

- ➢ **Sound** – cars arriving, doors creaking, footsteps on gravel, cat. Directional sound. Music built up suspense and tension, as would be loud suddenly when there was a shock moment. In dance scene music had heartbeat, creating scary atmosphere. Distortions in the music show time passing.

- ➢ **Costume** – simple. Nana = long grey skirt, white shirt and cream cardigan (conveyed age well). Emily = red trousers, white jumper (for majority of play). Dennis – brown suit, white shirt and dull tie (displayed his serious character). Simple costumes allowed quick change for Nana (rolled out of coffin) when turns into Emily spirit. Long black coat for ghost – covered Dennis costume easily for quick change

- ➢ **Shock moments** – Nana stood on sofa with blanket held up, ghost appears behind. Ghost stood behind gauze (audience couldn't see), light came on behind gauze, mask glowed. Emily had spirit and body. Doors closing in on Emily when ghost drugs her. Not too many, spaced with comedy elements allowing audience to relax.

- ➢ Very enjoyable. Excellent production all round. Three talented actors.

Sample question 1

Discuss the ways in which **TWO** performers used their skills in **ONE** production that you have seen.

Ideas for planning

• Start by giving the basic details of the production: title, playwright, company, venue and date. Give a general overview of the production: its genre, style, what you perceived its aims to be, especially in relation to the performance style. Were the performers playing just one role each, was it multi-role, was it physical theatre? Were any specialist skills required: mime, mask work, clowning etc?

• Discuss the directorial interpretation of the play and how this might have affected the demands placed upon the performers. Follow this with a more specific look at the interpretation of character offered by the two performers you have chosen. When discussing your observations about different elements of the performers' skills, pick out specific moments from the play to give detailed examples of each skill you are explaining. This will keep you focused and prevent your discussion from becoming too vague.

• Discuss in detail the physical skills employed by the two performers: movement, gesture, mime and facial expressions. What did these communicate?

• Discuss their use of space.

• Discuss in detail the vocal skills employed by the two performers: diction, pitch, tone, accent, projection etc.

• Discuss in detail the specific use of specialist skills: acrobatics, stage combat etc. Discuss the performers' use of costume, make-up, props and accessories. How did this add to the performance?

• Discuss the interaction between your two performers and others on stage, including the establishment of character relationships.

• If appropriate, look at the nature of ensemble playing.

• Discuss how the performers created emotions on stage and evoked (or not) an emotional response from the audience.

• Discuss the nature of their rapport with the audience.

• Finish by giving a brief assessment of ways in which the performers used their skills (note that the question here only asks for a discussion of their skills not an assessment, but it will do no harm to give a brief assessment and make a suitable finish to the essay).

Sample question 2

Choose **ONE** production that you have seen and assess the effectiveness of the set and costume designs.

Ideas for planning

• Start by giving the basic details of the production: title, playwright, company, venue and date. Give a general overview of the production: its genre, style, what you perceived its aims to be, especially in relation to the use of design.

• Since you are being asked to assess the effectiveness of these elements, it is useful to begin by outlining what you believe the director's intentions were. This will allow you to look carefully at how the set and costumes fitted into achieving these intentions and how successful they were in doing so. You need to be able to explain why you thought they were (or weren't) effective.

• Discuss in general the way in which the designs enhanced the mood and atmosphere of the production. Establish what the mood and atmosphere was and explain how the designs contributed to these.

• Describe the setting. Draw and label a sketch of the main set design.

• Assess the use and creation of space through levels, platforms etc. What did they achieve?

• Assess the methods used for transitions between scenes – revolves, trucks, flying etc. What did they contribute to the overall production?

• Assess the effectiveness of the establishment of location and period through set design. Establish which period is represented and what location is involved. What features of the design reflect this? How do the designs help create a feeling of place?

• Assess the effectiveness of the use of scale, shape, texture, colour and materials in the set design. How did these elements work together?

• Describe and assess the effectiveness of the overall intentions of the costume design – style, period, location and effect on audience. Draw sketches if appropriate.

• Assess the effectiveness of the use of colour, texture and fabric in the costume design. What do these achieve?

• Assess the effectiveness of the costumes in establishing character. Don't just describe costumes vaguely with adjectives such as 'prim', 'serious' or 'provocative': explain what you mean with reference to features such as cut, neckline, length and fit. The examiner should be able to visualise them.

• Assess the use made by the actors of their costumes.

• Assess the combined effectiveness of the costumes and set, and the effect on the audience. How did they complement each other? What effect did they have on the audience?

 ## Test yourself

1. With reference to one production that you have seen, discuss the ways in which the performers established their characters on stage through vocal and physical work.

2. Choose one production that you have seen in which the costume design made a strong contribution to the overall impact, and explain why it was so effective.

3. With reference to one production that you have seen, discuss the ways in which the director's interpretation was revealed to the audience.

4. Assess the contribution of the lighting and sound designs to the success or failure of one production that you have seen.

Theatre in Practice – Practitioners

Stanislavski

Why study Stanislavski?

Konstantin Stanislavski (1863–1938) is considered by many to be the most important practitioner for actors, as he is responsible for creating a system of rehearsal techniques that allow the actor to create a character in which both they and the audience can believe. Much of what an actor does today, when working on any naturalistic piece of theatre, is down to Stanislavski. So although much of what we will look at in this chapter seems obvious to us now, it is only so because Stanislavski felt the desire and need to work out a rehearsal method for himself in his own struggle to become a better actor.

It is important to remember that this is a series of rehearsal techniques and not a system for performance. The exercises and structures that will be referred to must be looked at in the context of preparation to play a role, and are not how an actor thinks when in front of an audience. It is with this process that we will be most concerned.

It is also important to understand that Stanislavski's system evolved over a great many years, during which he was constantly refining his ideas and working practices; indeed, he was still doing so at the end of his life. Much of Stanislavski's early work on psycho-technique, whereby the actor works from the inside out, allowing a psychological truth to instruct the physicality of a role, was altered in later years when he began work on the Method of Physical Action, whereby truthful actions lead to an emotional truth. We will return to these terms later in the chapter in more detail.

Background

Stanislavski was born Konstantin Sergeyevich Alekseyev into a wealthy bourgeois family in Moscow who were involved in amateur theatricals. His first performance came at the age of seven, and a few years later his father converted one wing of their country house into a small theatre. It was while appearing in a number of plays in this theatre that Stanislavski began to be consciously concerned with the art of acting. Indeed, after his first performance he realised that, although he had copied a well-known actor of the day in every detail, he had been completely inaudible and his hands had been in such constant motion that the audience had not been able to understand what he was saying.

His response to these early problems was to keep a notebook, in which he recorded his reactions to his work, tried to analyse where he was having difficulties and attempted to work out solutions. He continued to do this throughout his life. It is from these notebooks that the three books that relate his ideas are taken: *An Actor*

Further reading

Key texts to look at when studying Stanislavski are his *An Actor Prepares* (Methuen 1980), *Building a Character* (Methuen 1979) and *Creating a Role* (Methuen 1998).

Bourgeois is another way of saying middle-class.

See *My Life in Art* (Methuen 2001), the autobiography of Stanislavski's early years. It is important though when reading *My Life in Art* that you do not take everything he says as truth; it was partly written as a propaganda for his later theories and thus is not completely objective.

Prepares, *Building a Character* and *Creating a Role*, the latter two of which were published after his death.

An Actor Prepares, which has become something of a bible for actors, is written as fiction, in which the student Kostya is taken through a series of masterclasses with his tutor Tortsov. In reality Stanislavski is both of these characters.

Russian theatre before Stanislavski

It is important to understand the sort of theatre that was being produced in Russia in the mid 19th century and against which Stanislavski wished to rebel. Authoritarian managements produced plays in order to make a quick profit. Actors had little or no input into the creative process and were expected merely to imitate the actor who had first played the role. Acting was declamatory, melodramatic and wooden. Actors learnt stock positions and gestures to represent emotions (a hand on the heart to represent love, for example). Stanislavski called this mechanical acting. The rehearsal period was kept as short as possible (as no money was coming in during this time), and a prompter fed the actor the lines, leading to imitation. Flats and furniture were taken from stock, costumes were stereotyped to character and audiences expected nothing more.

Mechanical acting

Declamatory in this sense means to deliver lines loudly and with no attempt to sound natural.

Stanislavski grew to hate this stilted and sterile form of acting. He wanted to establish a theatre where actors created emotionally and physically truthful characters in which the audience could believe. He wanted to create realism in the theatre. He defined realism as 'selecting only those elements which revealed the relationships and tendencies lying under the surface'. In other words he wanted his actors to give their characters a motivation for their actions.

Realism

Stanislavski, *An Actor Prepares*.

In 1897 Stanislavski and Vladimir Nemirovich-Danchenko created Russia's first fully professional theatre, which was financed by private patronage and through general subscription. It was open all year round, offering high-quality drama. Great importance was placed on the script and the actors, while also focusing on realism in the sets, props and costumes. Their production of *The Seagull* by Chekhov in 1898 transformed the play, which had been a disaster in its first production. Stanislavski introduced details of real life, building on the simple stage directions to create a tense and moody atmosphere. The aim was to draw the audience further into Chekhov's universe of frustration and regret, through the truthful emotions and actions of the performers. This was the psychological realism of performance that Stanislavski was looking for. Although the literati liked the production, it was not a great success. Chekhov was not pleased with the result as he felt the play was more comedic than Stanislavski had made it. In addition, the production was a financial disaster. The general public did not appreciate this new approach to theatre and the actors found it hard to cope with the new performance style.

The Seagull

It was because of these early, failed attempts at direction that Stanislavski began work on his system of actor training. He was not aiming to produce a set of rules on how to act, but rather a means by which he could guide actors to find their own way into a character.

Key concepts

The fundamental aim

> "There can be no true art without living, it begins where feeling comes into its own. "
>
> *An Actor Prepares*

Stanislavski defined the fundamental aim of his system as 'to create the life of a human spirit, but also to express it in a beautiful artistic form'. He accepted that in the theatre you could not just reproduce real life, as much of real life is tedious and uninteresting – an actor has to make the character interesting to an audience and thus 'beautiful' to watch. An audience should be drawn to the character, become involved in their life and thus emotionally attached to them. The only way to achieve this was to give the character a psychological truth, but to choose those moments in a character's life that were sufficiently important and interesting to be attractive to watch.

The psycho-technique

Stanislavski recognised the problem that an actor has in working from the subconscious. If something is in our subconscious how do we make use of it without making the conscious version of it stilted and false? Much of the early part of his system, the psycho-technique, is based around solving this conundrum. His intention was that 'through conscious means we reach the subconscious'.

At the start Stanislavski understood that if an actor were to become a skilled craftsman then they would need daily training. He recognised also that the main tool that the actor has is their body, including the voice. Thus he set up a series of daily exercises in gymnastics, fencing, singing and dancing. Although gymnastics is no longer taught in most drama schools the other three still are. Serious actors will keep going to classes in movement and voice-work on a regular basis to keep themselves honed for when work comes along.

Be, don't show

Stanislavski wanted his audience to believe in everything that the character does on stage. You should not be able to see the acting going on, but should relax into accepting the actor as that character. It is important therefore that the actor does not show their emotions or situation to the audience through surface actions. The simplest exercise to work on this is to do some 'door' work. Most characters you are likely to play will make an entrance onto the stage at some point. As an actor you must know where your character has come from, what happened there and why you are coming into the new space.

Practise coming through a door in the following situations:

- You are coming back into your warm house after a long, cold walk
- You are leaving the headteacher's office after a serious telling-off
- You have just been told that you have got the main role in a new play, a part you desperately wanted to play
- You have just told your boyfriend/girlfriend that you are dumping them after three years together, because you have found someone else.

Try to take away as much physical action as possible. Don't plan anything. Don't try to give your audience clues in the way that you react to the situation, just think yourself into the situation and see what happens. Even if the audience doesn't pick up the complete situation they should get an idea of your mood and that is enough.

In the previous exercise you were playing the subtext, the motivation only. After all it is likely that the text will give the audience the rest.

Subtext

 Try the following exercises to see what effect subtext can have on acting.

Sweep the floor. Now sweep the floor as if you had to do it as a punishment. Next do the same task, but as if you were a barefoot dancer who is about to give a performance.

In pairs, talk about the weather, firstly as two spies who are passing on secret information, then as two people who are secretly in love but talking in front of other people. Try it as two people who can't stand each other but are forced to be together at a business convention.

You should notice that although the action (text) is the same in each situation, the subtext means that the action will be performed in very different ways. Stanislavski summed this up by saying 'whatever happens on stage must be for a purpose'. It is the purpose that makes an action interesting for an audience to watch.

Given circumstances

The given circumstances are the jumping-off point for an actor whenever they are given a role to play. These can be defined most simply as the facts that cannot be altered by the actor, anything over which the actor has no control. These include: the story of the play; the events, period, time and place of the action; the conditions of life; the director's and designer's interpretations; the scenery, costume, properties, lighting and sound effects – all those conditions which the actor must take into account.

If the play is set in the living room of your character, for instance, then you have to accept the set design as being the way your character would choose to decorate their living space. The costume that you are given to wear must be one that your character would choose to wear, even if as an actor you hate the colour. The director may have interpreted the play in a very different way from you but as an actor you have to go along with the director. An actor thus needs to do research. They must understand the world in which their character lives, especially if it is a very different world from their own.

Stanislavski took the idea of the given circumstances from Pushkin, a great Russian poet, who, when commenting on theatre, stated that 'sincerity of emotions, feelings that seem true in given circumstances, that is what we ask of a dramatist'. Stanislavski felt that this also applied to the actor. 'Sincerity of emotions' refers to emotions that the actor can understand and make the audience believe in. This does not mean that you have to have experienced exactly the same emotions as your character, but something similar that you can make work for you. We will return to this idea when looking at emotion memory.

Imagination

Magic IF

Having found the given circumstances of a role, the next stage is to supplement the information found with imagination. The first stage in this process is the Magic IF. The actor begins by considering the question: 'If I were in this situation, what would I *do*?'

> "IF acts as a lever to lift us out of the world of actuality into the realm of imagination."
>
> *An Actor Prepares*

The Magic IF acts as a key to unlock the actor's imagination, to enter the world of the character. By first asking the question 'what would I *do* in this situation?' the resulting actions will be true to you as an actor and therefore be more believable to an audience. By then placing your actions in the context of the given circumstances, you will be able to find truthful actions for the character in which you can believe.

Stanislavski wrote that:

> 'Truthful action arises from the actor's capacity to transform the conventions of the play and even crude theatrical lies into an artistic reality, through his own ability to make believe, no matter how fantastic or unlikely the play.' *An Actor Prepares*

The actor here can be likened to a child at play. Children have vivid imaginations, and can accept any situation and play it out with full belief. Thus an actor needs to rediscover this ability.

 Try the following exercises to develop the ability to 'play' and overcome self-consciousness.

- Cross the room as though it were a raging river with only a few large stones to give you safety
- Wrestle a cushion as though it were an alligator
- Walk across the room as though you were on the moon.

There should be no embarrassment or awkwardness about this. Just accept the situation as a child would and think yourself into the situation, and the actions will come naturally and believably.

> "The aim of the actor should be to use his technique to turn the play into a theatrical reality. In this process imagination plays by far the greatest part."
>
> *An Actor Prepares*

Some people say they have no imagination. This is not the case. Your imagination can be trained, just like your memory or your singing ability. It is vital for an actor to improve their imagination, in order to play roles further and further away from themselves.

The given circumstances are not enough to allow the actor to create a fully-rounded character. The playwright and director can show the actor the important aspects of a character, but to make a character 'real' the actor must use their imagination to fill in everything that is missing: the life off-stage, before and after the play, the nitty-gritty of that character's life. It is often helpful to do a 'day in the life' of your character. We said earlier that a play will only show the interesting parts of the character's life, but as an actor you should know the day-to-day banalities of that existence as well.

Exercises to help train your imagination:

- Create a story from the following list of words. You must use each word in order:
Biscuit, light bulb, Texas, pineapple, expertly, cardboard, Jupiter, eating, camel, pink

- Find resemblances between objects and people, for example: if Tony Blair was a sports car he would be a…

- Sit on a chair, but imagine it as a: block of ice, a hot stove, a porcupine

- Imagine you are a tree (so we *do* do that in drama!) and describe what you can see around you. The thought process here should not be 'I *am* a tree' but '*If* I *were* a tree…'.

> If you speak any lines, or do anything, mechanically, without fully realising who you are, where you came from, why, what you want, where you are going and what you will do when you get there, you will be acting without imagination.
>
> *An Actor Prepares*

All this will help you to fulfil Stanislavski's intention that 'every movement you make on the stage, every word you speak, is the result of the right life of your imagination'.

Observation

Along with imagination goes observation. As an actor you must observe everything and everyone around you. When you pass a couple arguing in the street, observe the way they are arguing and then fill in the gaps from your imagination as to the reason behind that argument. Treat it as an acting exercise and try to recreate that argument later with a colleague. Start from the point you observed and then work backwards and forwards from that point until you have created the play of that couple. Ensure that you are working from the given circumstances and develop the rest from your imagination, but keep the result as truthful as you can. It is important that in daily life you are observant of all around you and allow that to feed your imagination.

Attention and concentration

To make the best use of all that you have done so far, you must be able to maintain attention and concentration when on stage. The one place where an actor must not focus is on the audience, because in Stanislavski's theatre there is a fourth wall present between the stage and the audience. However, it is important that an actor does have a focus as otherwise an audience will feel that they are 'dead behind the eyes'. Even as a spear-carrier at the back of a large crowd, it is very noticeable to an audience if you have glazed over and switched off. And so, on what should the actor focus?

Circles of attention

Stanislavski suggests there are different kinds of attention, which he terms circles of attention. The first of these is the outer level. This is where an actor must focus on the objects or people around them on stage. The actor chooses the objects – which may include themselves – on which the character's focus should be at any point in the play. They then imagine a circle or beam of light coming down and illuminating just that object. The imagined light allows the actor to really focus on that object and observe it in all its detail. These beams of light are continuously going on and off as the focus of attention changes. The actor should be in a state of mind that Stanislavski called 'solitude in public': although in the presence of other people, the circle of light divides you from them and allows for full concentration. Remember as always that this is a rehearsal method, not something to be done in performance, as by then this should all be instinctive and in the subconscious mind of the actor.

There is also the inner level of attention, whereby the actor focuses on the inner life of their character and their given circumstances. This prevents the actor's own private concerns getting in the way of their performance. It is an example of the actor's cliche 'leave your problems at the stage door'. Stanislavski suggests that because so much of an actor's work is conducted in the realm of imagination, this inner attention is of particular importance.

Finally there is the outer-world level of attention. This is a focus on the way the world has affected your character – how history, religion, culture and the day-to-day life of the community your character exists in have affected their response to objects around them. In order to work on this an actor must be aware of their own responses to such things and have a deeper understanding of the world around them. Stanislavski's example is that of a chandelier being the object of attention. If you know that the chandelier once hung in Napoleon's own rooms does it alter the way you look at it from when you thought it was just an old, rather battered chandelier? By focusing on human nature and observing how other people respond to objects and ideas an actor will improve their own intuitive way of responding, thus allowing for a greater understanding of how any character they are playing will respond.

Relaxation An actor must learn to relax their whole body. In any performance an actor will have to move in a consciously different way from normal, in order to present a physical statement about the character. This will naturally create tension in the body and muscles, which an actor must be able to control. The tension of performance will also affect the actor. Nerves and anxiety will increase tension and will cause problems for breathing and therefore the voice will become strained. The actor must therefore learn a system of relaxation in order to get rid of this unwanted tension.

Units and objectives

When working on a role it is difficult at first to get a grasp of the whole character and their journey through the play. If every action must have a purpose, how can you work towards finding the purpose for each action? Stanislavski's solution was to break the role down into a number of small units and work on each unit separately to find its purpose (objective) before moving on. His analogy was that of eating a turkey, you have to carve the turkey into small pieces to eat – you couldn't put the whole turkey in your mouth at once.

Units A unit is described as a piece of text that contains an independent action, without which the unit could not exist. The smaller the unit, the easier the starting point. For instance, the first unit for a character might be opening the door and entering the room. What the actor needs to find is the character's objective for doing that action. Why does the character choose to open the door and enter the room? The answer must come in the form of an active verb and fit the phrase 'I wish to…'. This then is the motivation for the action.

Each unit should have a barrier, something the character wishes to overcome, so that there is an objective for getting through the unit. This could be a physical objective as in the case above – 'I wish to open the door and enter the room' – but it will always be more interesting for the audience if the objective is a psychological one – maybe 'I wish to open the door and enter the room silently so that I can steal the money kept inside because I am starving'. These objectives must be truthful to the character so that both you and the audience can believe in them.

Objectives

To find the different levels of objectives, try the following exercise:

- Greet your friend by shaking hands with them. This objective is merely mechanical and holds very little interest.

- Hold out your hand to your friend to show them that you love and respect them. This is more interesting but still quite straightforward.

- Yesterday you had a row with your friend. Hold out your hand to them to show that you wish to admit that you were wrong and are apologising. This is the truly psychological objective and therefore the most creative and difficult to achieve, while at the same time most likely to gain your audience's interest.

Stanislavski suggested that each unit should be given a name that encompasses both the action of the unit and the objective. By giving the unit this name the actor will always be aware, when rehearsing, of the character motivation behind the scene.

This division of the play into units is only temporary, to be viewed as another rehearsal method for the actor. As rehearsals progress the units should be joined together to form larger units, each of which should then be given a new objective to encompass all the actions within that section of text. Eventually the actor should be able to connect all the units together in order to decide what the character's objective is for the whole play. This is called the main objective, though Stanislavski also called it the super-objective. This is the one thing that your character is trying to achieve throughout the play and towards which all the separate parts of the play are leading. It may be that your character does not succeed in achieving their super-objective and this is certainly true in many plays. It is important to note that the super-objective cannot be achieved at any point in the play except at the end (or at your character's final appearance). Thus in *Macbeth*, for example, Macbeth's super-objective cannot be to become king because although this will get you through the first two acts of the play you are then left with a problem thereafter. One possibility is to consider that he wishes to ensure his children become king after him; this gives him motivation for all he does until his death. Each actor who plays the role may well come up with a different super-objective: this is why it becomes fascinating to watch different actors play such a role and why every production is unique.

The super-objective

Stanislavski also uses the term super-objective to refer to the playwright's main intention in writing the play. He discusses the director's need to find the super-objective of their interpretation, which should encompass the main theme of the play. It is the director's responsibility to ensure that all the characters in the play are working towards this super-objective. For example, if the director decides that the main theme of Chekhov's *Three Sisters* is to show the frustration of the sisters' lives, they have to make sure this theme is brought out in the production through the overall style of the performance. Each actor must choose an objective for their character that allows their frustration and regret to be revealed to the audience.

The through line of action

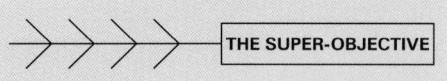

This is how Stanislavski visualised the through line of action.

Having chosen your super-objective, you now have to ensure that all previous objectives of the smaller units of the play are leading towards the super-objective in what Stanislavski called a 'through line of action'. If, on reworking the play, you discover that some unit objectives do not fit this, they will have to be changed.

The unbroken line

 Try to remember everything that you have done today by working back from this point to the moment you woke up.

Do this in minute detail; try to think yourself through every action and every conversation. Having done this, try working forward from the present moment into the future of your day, what will you be doing later? Create the conversations you might have.

In reality, life is a completely unbroken line; we know exactly what we have done and are doing minute by minute. On stage, it is the artistic imagination of the playwright that creates the line of your character in the likeness of truth. But the playwright only gives it to us in bits and pieces. We are not often told what happened before the play started, or exactly what the character was doing between Acts I and II. The actor has to fill in the missing sections of their character's life. This will add depth and truth to the character and allow for greater belief from the audience.

Justification of a role

Stage truth

Throughout this chapter we have been saying that it is the actor's responsibility to get the audience to believe in their character, to accept that they have become someone else. In order to achieve this the performance must be truthful. The actor must believe in their portrayal of the role. Clearly this cannot be a literal truth. Both the actor and the audience know that the actor is acting, that they are not really the character up on stage. What we are aiming for is the 'willing suspension of disbelief'. The audience, after all, wishes to believe in the character: they are on our side. It is only when the actor has no real belief in their role that the audience will also doubt in their existence.

The expression 'willing suspension of disbelief' was coined by English poet S.T. Coleridge (1772–1834) and applied to poetry, but it has mostly been used in discussions of drama.

In real life we do not think about our objectives all the time. We work instinctively; our objectives are just there, so they are of course true. On stage actors repeat actions each night and therefore only the first time could possibly be true. In repetition we get a false imitation of an action. So how do actors go about recreating truth? Stanislavski defines the difference between truth and stage truth as follows:

> 'In ordinary life, truth is what really exists, what a person really knows. Whereas on the stage it consists of something that is not actually in existence, but which could happen.' *An Actor Prepares*

By working from the inside and using all the elements discussed above, an actor can create a character that has a sense of truth. This is defined as the justification of the role.

 Even the simplest of actions must be detailed and have a justification in order to make them believable. Try the following actions:

- Make a bed
- Thread a needle
- Scramble eggs.

Unless these things are full of the minute details behind carrying them out in real life, and have a purpose, they will not be believable. By doing this you achieve physical truth. It is these small physical actions that can really illuminate a role and make the larger tragedies of drama seem more convincing.

Actors must also consciously think about the physical actions required of a role, once the groundwork on the inner life of the character has been achieved. Stanislavski was aware that even if the inner life is understood in great depth, if it does not lead to truthful actions the character will not be believed by the audience. They can only see the outer life and must rely on that for their stage truth. However, if the actor only thinks about the outer life and has no understanding of the inner life, then the actions will have no basis in reality and be seen as false by the audience.

This constant conflict between the conscious and the subconscious led Stanislavski to create possibly the most controversial element of his system – emotion memory. This is at the heart of the psycho-technique. Stanislavski felt that whenever an actor needed to portray an emotion on stage they should not try to invent or create an emotion that was alien to them. This would only lead to a false emotion, which would get in the way of stage truth. Thus the actor should look into their past and make use of their own memories to find similar feelings and emotions from their own life to use on stage.

Just as you can reconstruct in your visual memory an image of some long-forgotten place, person or thing, so too your emotion memory can be used to bring back feelings you have already experienced. It is commonly thought that everything we have ever experienced is kept within our memory as if it were in a bank or library, and all we have to do to recover the lost memory is to find the way to make a withdrawal. You have probably experienced the feeling of coming across an old toy in the attic and finding memories flooding back of occasions when you played with that toy. It is extraordinary what comes back; images of the clothes

> " We use the conscious technique of creating the physical body of a role and by its aid achieve the creation of the subconscious life of the spirit of the role. "
>
> *An Actor Prepares*

Emotion memory

people were wearing, even the conversations that you had at the time.

Stanislavski's use of emotion memory requires the actor to open their emotional library and is thus an exercise not to be treated lightly. It is an intensely personal thing and can take time. Therefore it is more a private rehearsal technique, though a sensitive director can assist the actor to find the relevant emotions. Of course, sometimes the actor may not think they have a suitable emotion to draw upon, for example in the case of playing a murderer on stage, but there is always some emotion that can be emphasised and magnified to get close to the desired feeling. In the case of the murderer, for example, if the murder is the result of great anger or jealousy, then an occasion when the actor was angry or jealous in their own life can be found and made use of.

In fact, what the actor is really looking for is the physical reaction to the relevant emotion. Remember what we said about stage truth being to do with physical actions? In order to be believable on stage when expressing emotion the actor must have the correct physical reaction to that emotion. It is another example of the use of Magic IF. What would I do if I was feeling that emotion?

So how does the actor go about finding the relevant reaction to the relevant emotion? It is difficult to remember immediately in any detail those big occasions in life when emotions come into play, so the key to the re-creation is to remember the small details of the moment and build them up into the whole picture. For instance, thinking about your reaction to the first time you fell in love is unlikely to give you much physical information. The way forward is to remember where you were at the time, what was in the room, the colours and smells of the occasion, the words that were spoken, the music that might have been playing. All of these things will allow you to build up the overall memory and lead you to your physical reaction at the time. The answer is in using your five senses.

 From each of the following starting points try to recreate a memory by building the complete picture of a specific moment in your life relating to each of the following:

- Remember the first time you saw waves crashing on the shore
- Remember a time when you heard wind howling though trees; or listened to a sad song
- Remember the taste of mustard; of marmite
- Remember the feeling of an injection; the feeling of having your hair washed
- Remember the smell of newly mown grass; a bad egg.

What was the physical effect of each of these memories? You should have found that a very clear reaction took place, which you can now recreate. Which sense gave the most immediate and powerful reaction? Most people find that smell has the strongest effect – which is why the perfume industry is so successful.

The effect of all this is that we find truthful physical actions resulting from emotions; truthful because we created them subconsciously when we went through that emotion in real life. As an actor we can then recreate the physical reaction to the desired emotion when required by the character. Obviously when performing a role you cannot go through this process in performance for every emotion. This is a rehearsal method that takes time, but which does produce results. Having found a truthful physical reaction we can recreate that action on stage without going through the painful process of digging up the emotion again.

Of course, this can be a dangerous process for an actor to go through and as we will see later, Stanislavski recognised this and found a different approach for creating truthful emotions on stage.

One important aspect of acting that this process highlights is that actors always remain themselves on stage, whatever their imaginary experiences are. Stanislavski said that, 'the moment you lose yourself on stage marks the departure from truly living your part and the beginning of exaggerated false acting'. This explains why an actor, no matter how good, cannot play every role ever written. There are some roles you are just not suited to because of who you are.

Communication between actors

Up to this point we have focused on the individual actor and how they prepare for a role. However, it is important to remember that a play is a team effort, requiring highly complicated communication between actors. Actors who speak their own lines, however truthfully, cannot remain truthful if, when waiting for their next cue, they simply switch off and lose any focus they had. Listening and responding – re-acting if you like – is as important as speaking.

Stanislavski defined this form of communication as communion and stated that an actor must have communion at all times with something and someone. If actors are to grab the attention of the audience there must be an effort to maintain an uninterrupted exchange of feelings, thought and actions among themselves. The inner material for this exchange should be sufficiently interesting to hold spectators. In order to help his actors work on this he came up with the idea of visualising rays coming from their eyes and the ends of their fingers that would keep them in constant connection with someone or something. Actors must learn how to send out these rays and also how to receive them from others. There are three types of communion: direct communion with an object or person on stage; self-communion, when you are in discussion with yourself; and communion with an absent or imaginary object (for instance when thinking about a person who is not present on stage with you).

Adaptation is defined by Stanislavski in *An Actor Prepares* as 'the inner and outer means that people use in adjusting themselves to one another in a variety of relationships and also as an aid in affecting an object'. What this means is that as actors we must be able to adapt the way we behave to suit the people and circumstances around us.

> "Always and forever you must play yourself on stage, but it will be in an infinite variety of combinations of objectives, and given circumstances, which you have prepared for the part and which have been smelted down in the furnace of your emotion memory."
>
> *An Actor Prepares*

Communion

> "If an actor listens, he must both listen and hear. If he smells he must inhale. If he looks he must look and see, and not just glance at an object without hanging onto it, as it were, with his teeth."
>
> *An Actor Prepares*

Adaptation

Try the following:

Find a way to leave a class early, but only tell one person in the class that you are planning this. You must find a way that will convince both your teacher and your fellow pupils that your reason is genuine. That is your objective. Keep your eye always on the objective rather than entertaining yourself or your fellow classmate who is in the know. If the teacher is proving awkward, you will find you have to adapt your reasons and increase your efforts.

Actors must adapt all the aids that they are given from the text or by a director so that these become appropriate to the actors themselves and to their characters.

Forces and processes

Inner motive forces

Stanislavski suggests that there are three inner motive forces that an actor must develop in order to work through his system successfully. The combination of these three forces in an actor enables them to be as creative as possible:

➢ **Feeling.** An actor must be able to feel the role in order to be creative

➢ **Mind.** This initiates and directs creativeness

➢ **Will.** The actor must want to find artistic truth if they are to be creative.

Six principle processes

Stanislavski also divides the actor's art into six processes:

➢ **Will.** By getting to know the author's work the actor becomes enthusiastic about it and this enthusiasm arouses their creativity

➢ **Searching.** Through searching within and through external research, the actor can find the psychological material needed for creation

➢ **Experience.** The actor invisibly creates the inner and outer image of the character and experiences emotions as the character does

➢ **Physicalising.** The actor creates the character visibly by expressing feelings physically

➢ **Synthesis.** The actor brings together and merges the processes of experience and physicalising

➢ **The effect on an audience.** The actor adapts their performance where necessary to allow the audience to understand and appreciate the character.

The method of physical action

In later years Stanislavski became increasingly concerned that the psycho-technique was a long, slow process for an actor and could be very difficult to achieve. Some aspects of the system, such as emotion memory, were complex and indeed dangerous for an actor to undergo. They could lead to negative results: tension, exhaustion and hysteria. He became more and more dissatisfied with the mind/body split and wanted to see if the actor could work from the physical aspects of a role and find the emotional aspects in a safer manner.

Having broken down the creative process into so many elements and series of exercises, Stanislavski felt there was now a need to re-emphasise the overall qualities of a role.

He began to look at the way an actor would first approach a part. When reading the play aloud there would be initial impressions that an actor could not deny – they would be attempting to give reason and motivation to a role that they did not yet understand. Stanislavski felt there could be too much discussion at the start of rehearsals when an actor should be up 'on his feet' trying out the role. It was not good to be imposing ideas, making judgements about a role, many of which would have been given to the actor by a director. This, along with the worries about emotion memory, led him to try a system that began with the body rather than the mind.

Improvisation

Previously improvisation had been used only as a support to the psycho-technique, and physical action had come last. In this system physical action became the stimulus to awaken the imagination and the subconscious. The actor begins their creative work by improvising with the rest of the cast the sequence of actions that makes up the play. The director will have given the cast the details of the plot only, with limited information on the characters. The text is unseen at this stage and so the actors use their own words. The actor is still answering the question 'what would I do if...?', and linking the answer to the given circumstances, but now the actor is engaging his total being from the start, not just his mind. Thus the actors' physical actions are completely true to themselves. The actors therefore create a personalised through line of action and absorb the psychology of their characters into their actions, before seeing a single line of text. Once they receive the text they should be able to adapt their actions to suit the finer details of the character, resulting in a logical, coherent psychological life.

Tempo-rhythm

As part of the method of physical action, Stanislavski stressed the importance of finding an inner rhythm for the character. He discovered that if you found the correct rhythm for an action then this would lead to an emotional response, which would be just as believable as those discovered through emotion memory. Think of film music, where the rhythm and mood of the music often give the audience the emotion of a scene. Many films are pretty dull if you take away the music soundtrack and just keep the dialogue. Stanislavski is suggesting that while you are acting you should work with your own personal music soundtrack.

Try the following exercise using a metronome:

Get a tray, a number of cups and saucers and a teapot. You are a waiter serving tea in a posh restaurant. Set the metronome to a fast speed. Now serve the tea in the rhythm of the metronome. How does the rhythm affect the way you set down the cups and pour the tea? You may find that you become quite flustered, but what precise emotion comes to you as you do this? Now try the exercise with the metronome at various contrasting speeds. What is the difference when the pace is very slow? If you know that the character should be angry, which speed is most helpful in creating this emotion?

If you don't have access to a metronome get a friend to clap their hands or click their fingers at a consistent speed.

Having two metronomes and therefore two rhythms can extend this exercise. Use one rhythm as your outer pace and one to represent your inner feelings. For instance, you might be on your first day as a waiter, very nervous, but determined not to show it. Try a fast inner rhythm combined with a measured pace for your physical actions. This helps to develop a character with a subtext. You can even work with three or more rhythms where each speed represents a different set of thoughts and actions.

When rehearsing with a group try to ensure that everyone is working with a different set of rhythms. If a cast all work at the same rhythm the result can be very dull to watch, since it will seem as if there are no individuals on stage.

Don't worry if the exercise breaks down or you, or members of the group, suddenly start to laugh: this rhythm exercise can be stressful and laughter is just the release of the tension you may find builds up in you.

The role of the director

Most of what we have discussed so far is concerned with how an actor makes use of Stanislavski's system. However, we should also consider what the role of the director is in a Stanislavskian production. Clearly their major role is to facilitate the actors' use of the system and to ensure the overall realism of the production. In order to do this they must:

➢ Demand full discipline from the actors

➢ Help the actors with vocal and physical training as demanded by the play

➢ Ensure that each individual actor (and the company as a whole) achieves psychological realism through inner truth

➢ Initiate minute attention to detail, both in the performances and the design elements

➢ Ensure the play has an overall super-objective and that each actor's individual super-objective is consistent with this

➢ Evoke historical authenticity in a period play, from both the actors and the designers

➢ Guide the actors through the processes of the system.

Answering questions on Stanislavski

The main question on Stanislavski will ask you to explain what you understand by some of the terms in his system, to show how you would use them in rehearsal either as an actor or as a director and to assess their effectiveness. You are likely to be asked to discuss either one or two major terms, or two or three minor ones. You are being asked to show knowledge and understanding of the system as a rehearsal process and thus you need to show how it is used by the actor or director. It is helpful when answering as an actor to be able to refer to a particular character that you have played, or would like to play. However, it is important that you do not let your answer become a character study rather than focusing on Stanislavski's rehearsal methods. Similarly, if you are writing from the point of view of a director it will be helpful to refer to a particular play. Choose a naturalistic play you know well; this could be a set text such as *The Three Sisters* or *The Shadow of a Gunman*. But again, remember not to let this become a 'literary' essay about the play itself.

Sample question

Explain what you understand by Stanislavski's use of the terms 'Magic IF' and 'imagination', and show how you would use them when preparing a role for performance.

Ideas for planning

In your opening paragraph, briefly explain the overall point of Stanislavski's system for actors, the aim of gaining 'stage truth' and developing a character in which both the actor and audience can believe. State what character/play you will refer to throughout your essay. Then…

• Define each of the terms and show where they come in the system. Thus the Magic IF is a starting point after discovering all the given circumstances. Indicate how using the phrase 'what would I do if…' helps you to produce truthful physical actions, because they are true to you and thus will seem true to the audience.

• Give an example of a moment when you would find the use of Magic IF helpful while working on your chosen character. Give full details on the process involved.

• Refer to the need to open the subconscious and how the Magic IF does that by forcing you to look at the way you react to different situations. Show how you then adapt the reactions that were true to you in order to make them appropriate for the given circumstances. At all times give clear examples from your chosen character.

• Show how the Magic IF leads on to the general use of imagination to fill the gaps in the character that are not provided by the given circumstances. Show how you create those missing elements by searching your imagination, through observation, through research and through improvisation. Indicate how the more you use your imagination to build up the depth of your character through inner truth, the more believable your playing of the role will become.

Artaud

Why study Artaud?

Born in Marseilles, Antonin Artaud (1896–1948) started to write at an early age. However, he suffered from mental health problems throughout his life and these often led him to reject his previous work, destroying poems and other writings. He developed a drug addiction and found it difficult to maintain friendships and working relationships. During his lifetime he enjoyed very little success: his productions were flops; his writing, which included poetry and polemic, was often unvalued, and his ideas were marginalised. In the 1960s, directors led by Peter Brook revisited what Artaud had

Further reading

The key text to look at when studying Artaud is his *The Theatre and its Double* (Calder 1998).

written about, and found ideas there that supported what they were doing in their own new and alternative theatre.

Artaud represents the other end of the performance spectrum from Stanislavski. He did not want to represent reality in his productions: he wanted to transcend it. He did not want his actors to be limited by the representation of real people with real psychologies: he wanted them to open up completely new areas of experience, almost entirely divorced from the reality outside the theatre. He did not want to create productions which could be 'understood': he wanted to create productions that helped the audience to understand. That is why he became a kind of patron saint to those directors who needed some sort of authority to bless the experimental theatre and 'happenings' of the 1960s.

Theatrical context and political aims

Artaud instinctively joined with those artists and performers who rejected conservative and bourgeois theatre. With them, he demanded a theatre which challenged the audience and which opened their eyes to new ideas and new values. Theatre was like the plague: values and experiences change and experiences are sharpened when a group of people has to face up to new dangers. Artaud wanted a dangerous theatre, one capable of exploring extremes – what he called a cruel theatre.

Surrealism

His politics, implicit throughout his work, were the politics of anarchy and free-thinking. Initially, these were the politics, too, of the Surrealists. In 1925, for example, consistent with his loyalty to the Surrealist movement (which he had joined in 1924 following an invitation from its leader, French writer André Breton) Artaud wrote to the director of the Comédie Française insulting conventional theatre, and stating 'Molière is a twat'. Artaud – and the Surrealists – wanted to breathe fresh life into the theatre, using it not as a place for bourgeois entertainment, but as a place of dreams and emotional discovery.

> Molière (1622–1673) represented all that was orthodox and conservative in the theatre, not so much for what he'd written, but because of the status given to his comedies by bourgeois society. He had become a 'classic' and was therefore assumed to be beyond criticism.

Surrealism is thus an important influence on Artaud's work and ideas. Surrealists such as Tristan Tzara and Breton emphasised the importance of dreams in the apprehension of truth and reality. Dreams, they argued, went beyond reality: they were not just real, but were 'surreal'. In this they were mirroring, to some extent, the ideas of psychoanalyst Sigmund Freud whose work was gradually becoming popularised outside the German-speaking world. He saw dreams as a window onto the sub-conscious. What is more, Surrealists wanted a chaotic art that shocked its audience into thought and discovery.

Further study

Find out more about: the ideas and work of Sigmund Freud; the surrealist movement.

Pirandello

In 1921, aged 24, Artaud took his first part as an actor. He subsequently played a large number of small roles, including the prompter in the 1924 revival of Pirandello's modernist play *Six Characters in Search of an Author*. In this play, Pirandello develops the idea that characters 'come alive' in a playwright's mind and that, having been 'born' in such a way, go on to seek a story to tell. In the play, the characters reveal their story, through reflection and quarrels, in a way which seems surreal and uncontrolled. The play deals, on one level, with the differences between the 'real world'

> " In Europe, no one knows how to scream any more. "
> Antonin Artaud

and the 'imaginary world'. In hindsight, this text seems a significant place where a study of Artaud might begin, because of its mingling of the 'actual' with the 'imaginary' and because of its rejection of the bourgeois expectations of an 'entertaining' but unchallenging theatre.

As a performer himself, Artaud found more success as an actor in the cinema than in the theatre. The impact of film and cinema on Artaud's thinking is clearly important. He later developed ideas about the theatre which emphasised the use of the most modern equipment and effects, much of which, like electric lighting and sound recording, were still very much in their infancy. This emphasis on light and sound effects stems surely from an observation of their effect in the films of the day. On the other hand, he came to see cinema as ultimately limited.

Compose a letter to a newspaper.

Adopt the role of a theatre-goer disenchanted with the populist and expensive nature of West End shows. Argue that the West End is not the place to see 'real theatre'.

Productions and projects, successes and failures

It is a little misleading, perhaps, to refer to Artaud as a 'practitioner'. His own work in the theatre was limited both in scope and success. He never had the financial support to be able to put his ideas into practice without compromise, and the compromises – such as the use of inappropriate theatres and of under-rehearsed companies – led to the productions failing.

In 1926, Artaud founded the Alfred Jarry Theatre with two colleagues, Robert Aron and Roger Vitrac. The company was conceived as a society for the presentation of occasional performances, of which there were a total of eight between 1927 and 1929 in three different theatres, usually with one rehearsal only on stage.

Alfred Jarry was a young French writer whose play in 1896 *Ubu roi ou les Polonais* had a lasting impact on alternative French theatre. This was an eccentric play, more like a revue, eccentrically staged on a single set without the use of a curtain – both extraordinary departures from the normal practice of the day. 'The intention,' says J.L. Styan, 'was not so much to amuse the audience as to insult it.' By naming his project after Jarry, Artaud was attaching himself and his colleagues to a clearly alternative and anarchic tradition.

The first programme of the Alfred Jarry Theatre, in 1927, included three works. Artaud's (called *Acid Stomach or the Mad Mother*) included a young man in almost complete darkness, moving a chair forward then back, uttering mysterious phrases as he did so. A later piece, *The Spurt of Blood*, included human limbs and pieces of masonry falling from the flies to represent the collapse of civilisation.

In 1928, Artaud staged the first French production of Strindberg's *A Dream Play*. Strindberg's early dramas, such as *Miss Julie* (1888), share with Ibsen's major works a preoccupation with psychological realism. These plays invite a Stanislavskian approach to character

Film

Between 1922 and 1935 Artaud appeared in over twenty films, notably Gance's *Napoleon* (as Marat) and Dreyer's *The Passion of Joan of Arc* (as the young monk, Massieu). He argued that silent films were much to be preferred to talkies.

> One cannot compare a cinema image, however poetic it may be, since it is restricted by the film, with a theatre image which obeys all life's requirements.

Antonin Artaud, 'The Theatre of Cruelty (First Manifesto)' in *The Theatre and its Double* (Calder 1998).

Alfred Jarry Theatre

J.L. Styan, *Modern Drama in theory and practice: symbolism, surrealism and the absurd* (Cambridge University Press 1983).

development and discovery. However, towards the end of his life, Strindberg turned to writing short, poetic pieces that employed symbolism and surrealism. Such plays as *A Dream Play* (1902) and *The Ghost Sonata* (1907) not only exemplified a theatrical development of the ideas of the symbolists and the surrealists, but also looked forward to expressionism and the theatre of the absurd. In such works, Strindberg discovered for himself – without any knowledge of Freud's work – how dreams may reveal personality, character traits, obsessions and fears. As such, these works of Strindberg are in harmony with Artaud's thinking and can be seen in some ways as companion pieces to his theoretical writings. What Artaud liked about The Ghost Sonata was the way in which 'the real and unreal merge, as they do in the mind of someone falling asleep.'

Artaud, quoted in *The Director and the Stage* by Edward Braun (Methuen 1982). A student of Artaud ought to be familiar with these works by Strindberg.

'There is no more firmament'

This scenario, prepared for the stage by Artaud, appears in his *Collected Works*. A short extract from the opening three pages is presented here.

See *Collected Works*, Antonin Artaud, tr. Victor Corti (Calder 2000). For more on scenarios, and why Artaud used them, see page 125.

> Darkness. Explosions in the dark. Harmonies cut short. Raw sounds. Sound blurring. The music gives the impression of a far-off cataclysm; it envelops the theatre, falling as if from a vertiginous height. Chords are struck in the sky; they dissipate, going from one extreme to the other. Sounds fall as if from a great height, stop short and spread out in arcs, forming vaults and parasols. Tiered sounds.
>
> Beginnings of glimmers that change continually, passing from red to harsh pink, from silver to green, turn white; suddenly boundless, opaque, yellow light, the colour of dirty fog or the Simoon...
>
> Street cried. Various voices. An infernal racket. When one sound stands out, the others fade into the background accordingly...
>
> A hysterical woman wails, makes as if to undress. A child cries with huge, terrible sobs...
>
> Sudden stop. Everything starts again. Everyone takes his place again as if nothing had happened.

The Simoon is a strong, dry wind.

You can see from the scenario how Artaud does not discipline his imagination to produce something pragmatic. He uses a huge range of theatrical devices and machinery to achieve effects. These effects rely on metaphor to create meaning.

 Discuss how you could possibly present this text in performance.

You might wish to have a go at doing so. Discuss what you think the meanings of the piece are: how important is it that the various levels of meaning remain enigmatic and elliptic? Having identified some threads of meaning, try your own hand at producing a scenario that has a similar mood and purpose – what imagery would you use on stage today?

Ideas about theatre, actor, director

Effects

Artaud wanted theatre to bombard its audience with exaggerated and intense effects. He wanted to use all the technology available to support the performers in confronting the audience with challenging ideas and images. He was never sufficiently able to finance the production of his dreams, however, and too often was left to compromise in unsuitable venues with companies of actors whose enthusiasm for his ideas was lukewarm.

Just as he demanded the theatre to exaggerate its effects – blinding lights, amplified sound, symbolic staging – so he wanted actors to exaggerate their performances. Physically he demanded big gestures and the use of masks. He asked actors to speak so slowly or so quickly that language became meaningless and merely an auditory effect. He wanted actors to communicate huge emotions. He also had no wish that actors should 'be' their parts: all his work points to the primacy of metaphor over metonymy (see page 124). In auditioning for the part of a king in a conventional production, Artaud appeared on all fours, barking. This, he explained, was how he viewed the way the king behaved. It is a typical Artaud gesture, but he didn't get the part. Try to imagine the kind of audition performance which would get you a part in a play of Artaud's.

For six years, from 1929, addicted to drugs and living in poverty, Artaud did virtually no work in the theatre. The theoretical work behind his idea of a theatre of cruelty dates from this period. In the *First Manifesto* (1932), Artaud says that theatre will never be itself again, 'unless it provides the audience with truthful distillations of dreams where its taste for crime, its erotic obsession, its savageness... gush out'. In 1938, *The Theatre and its Double* – a collection of writings about the theatre – was published.

A clear understanding of what Artaud was trying to achieve in his theoretical work can be gained from considering the impact on him of two performances: one in 1922 by Cambodian dancers; the second a performance in 1931 of Balinese dance-drama at the Paris Colonial Exhibition. It is important to remember how distant Cambodia and Bali would have seemed in those pre-war years. Even now, Cambodia and Bali remain glamorous and exotic destinations. In the 1920s and 1930s, in the absence of television and so on, these performances would have appeared extraordinary to their audiences in a way which we cannot really now imagine.

Balinese dance-drama is essentially religious in nature. Tales of Hindu legend are enacted in a deeply spiritual and stylised way. Actors wear colourful and deeply unrealistic make-up as well as symbolic masks, intricately built up on their faces. Hand-gestures are used symbolically to convey mood and meaning. The performances, which are long and take place on holy days in the courtyards of temples, are given in local tongues and are accompanied by a gamelan, which is largely a percussion orchestra playing lines of interweaving rhythms. The audience is not spell-bound; they know the stories. For them, the telling is a sharing of a communal heritage, rather than a comfy entertainment.

Imagine the impact of this on Artaud. He had been exploring the effects of light and sound, of symbolic imagery, of using theatre to explore life's greatest mysteries. These performances offered him a whole new way of approaching these areas – performances founded in a long tradition utterly alien to the French theatre of Molière and Racine.

Actor's role

Balinese dance-drama

Artaud, quoted in *The Director and the Stage*.

Racine (1639–1699) wrote tragedies and was regarded with huge respect in France, like Molière: see page 25.

> Dialogue does not specifically belong to the stage but to books. I maintain the stage is a tangible, physical place that needs to be filled and it ought to be allowed to speak its own concrete language. "

Artaud 'Production and metaphysics' in *The Theatre and its Double* (Calder 1998).

It is also worth considering that for the Balinese performers, there is no author or director: there is tradition and there is performance and there is an audience.

Artaud noticed a number of key things about these performances, especially about the Balinese dancers. Firstly, there was a complete use of almost every theatrical ploy: visuals, sound, gesture, language and so on. Secondly, there was an impact far beyond sense. Ignorant of what is actually being said, the audience found themselves nonetheless drawn in to the absorbing drama of the performance. Artaud was impressed by the performance's independence from a merely verbal language. Thirdly, he recognised in the ritual nature of the performance a way of communicating deep spiritual truths. In short, Artaud confirmed for himself that meaning which cannot be summarised in language can have a deep effect. This, he claimed, is the true purpose of theatre. Just as Jarry had claimed many years before, Artaud argued that theatre is only true theatre when it offers something that cannot be offered by a novel, a poem or by any other medium.

It is important to remember that Artaud made no attempt to understand the Balinese theatre in the way the Balinese would have done. He knew that an understanding of the language, for example, or a familiarity with the story or with the significance of the gestures, would change the meaning of the performances. What he recognised is that the drama is more effective, more visceral, more meaningful, more engaging, without this cultural baggage. He wanted to devise drama which appeared to his audiences as the Balinese dance-drama appeared to him.

Try devising a ritual.

This could be a ritual for greeting a visitor, for blessing a marriage, for remembering the dead, for increasing the fertility of a garden, or for any one of a thousand other things. Invite other members of your group to act as witnesses to the ritual. You may not need to use a theatre or drama space, you may find a more appropriate venue elsewhere, perhaps even out of doors.

At the end of your ritual, your witnesses might write brief notes on what they have seen, and how they have interpreted it – as if they were visitors to Bali watching a temple play. Consider why your ritual may be most successful when there is least agreement about what it means.

Theatre of Cruelty

If we look at five key ideas behind Artaud's concept of a Theatre of Cruelty, we can see just how much they owe to this kind of interpretation of the Balinese performances.

1. Artaud argued against conventional theatre spaces. He associated these with bourgeois entertainment, with wealth and manners. Audiences in theatres offering this kind of entertainment do not want to develop spiritually, as Artaud wanted them to do. He wished to do away with stage and auditorium, and to replace these with a single location without any partitions of any sort. The audience should be clearly integrated within the performance, which he envisaged here as a kind of promenade performance. He recognised how the Balinese theatre gained some of its effect from being performed in an undecorated courtyard with the audience almost milling among the performers.

2. Artaud was opposed to representing 'real life' on stage. He emphasised the ritual nature of the performance and the way in which the audience is as much a part of this ritual as the performers.

3. Everything theatrical will be used to create a new language of the theatre. Language itself – the words of the script – will be subjugated to all the other devices available to the company:

> Shouts, groans, apparitions, surprise, dramatic moments of all kinds, the magic beauty of the costumes modelled on certain ritualistic patterns, brilliant lighting, vocal, incantational beauty, attractive harmonies, rare musical notes, object colours, the physical rhythm of the moves whose build and fall will be wedded to the beat of moves familiar to all, the tangible appearance of new, surprising objects, masks, puppets, many feet high, abrupt lighting changes, the physical action of lighting stimulating heat and cold, and so on.
> Antonin Artaud, 'The Theatre of Cruelty' in *The Theatre and its Double* (Calder 1998).

Artaud wanted every element of theatrical performance exaggerated beyond its normal use and meaning: brighter lights, more varied colours, language gabbled or slowed to a meaningless series of grunts, music as an object not as an accompaniment.

4. The actor must 'use his emotions in the same way as a boxer uses his muscles'. Artaud imagined heavy physical demands being made of his actors, who, through his emphasis on gesture and ritual, are almost dancers: 'The question of breathing is of prime importance; it is inversely proportional to external expression.' He wanted actors committed to his experimental approaches: 'Every emotion has an organic basis and an actor charges his emotional voltage by developing his emotions within him... In Europe no-one knows how to scream any more.' We shall see later on page 126 how the films of Derek Jarman share many ideas with Artaud. Jarman worked with a close company of actors who were all committed philosophically and emotionally to the project. This is one of Artaud's big demands of an actor. There must be a community spirit in which actors make unusual emotional and physical demands of themselves in a supportive environment.

Antonin Artaud, 'An Affective Athleticism' in *The Theatre and its Double* (Calder 1998).

5. The subject matter will focus on myths and well-known tales. It will disregard texts. When performances are built on existing texts, these texts will be torn apart into fragments and reassembled: 'Instead of harking back to texts regarded as sacred and definitive, we must first break theatre's subjugation to the text and rediscover the idea of a kind of unique language somewhere between gesture and thought... We will not act written plays but will attempt to stage productions straight from subjects, facts or known works.'

Artaud, 'An Affective Athleticism'.

Imagine you are asked to produce an Artaudian version of *The Tempest*.

As an example of the kind of material his new theatre would present, Artaud referred to making an adaptation of a Shakespearean work. In preparing for your production, think about these questions:

- Which elements of *The Tempest* make it suitable for this kind of treatment?

- How would a company go about treating the text to prepare such a production?
- Which scenes would be most effective? (And why? And how?)

Work on one scene and produce a Theatre of Cruelty version.

Metaphor and metonymy

For more on Stanislavski see pages 102–117.

The difference between Artaud and Stanislavski is the difference between metaphor and metonymy. It's very useful to see and understand this distinction. We need to be sure that we know what metaphor and metonymy are and we need to see how an understanding of their differences helps us grasp what Stanislavski and Artaud were seeking in their work. It is worth spending some time on this, because a philosophical understanding of the positions of these two practitioners will help us see precisely what their individual aims and intentions were.

Metonymy is the suggestion of a whole through the description of a part. Such use may become quite stylised, such as when a historian might talk about the 'crowned heads of Europe'. Here, the historian does not, of course, mean to refer just to one part of the body: indeed, they may be referring not only to the personages themselves, but to the whole aristocratic hierarchy that regulated European power.

What concerns us here is the use of metonymy to tell a story. We are familiar with this, although we may not realise we are. When we read about a character's bedroom, for example, we may read just a few details about it, which the novelist has chosen to reveal. Maybe there's a particular poster on the wall, maybe a dirty mug on a bedside table, maybe a dozen CDs scattered over the rug. We build up a picture not only of the room from these details, but of its occupant, too. Film directors use the same technique. Metonymy deals with parts. This is just like real life. We draw conclusions about our friends and colleagues from short conversations, brief glimpses, two or three hours together here and there. We may find, as time goes on, that our first impressions created the wrong picture, or at least we now want to revise it. We do this all the time.

This is why writers who employ metonymy feel 'realistic'. It is because they are creating meaning in their writing, using the very same technique that we use to create meaning in our lives. Stanislavski's exercises and training programmes are all designed to explore the relationship between the part and the whole. He takes the few words which a character is given, say in a Chekhov play, and through imagination, improvisation, exploration and so on he explores how these parts might relate to a whole. He wants his actors to have a complete sense of the whole of a character before they reveal the small part which Chekhov wants the audience actually to see.

Metaphor, on the other hand, is much more dangerous. Writers use metaphor to suggest ideas, rather than to define them. Metaphor makes the reader – the audience – do more work and to think more. In Kafka's short story *Metamorphosis,* Gregor Samsa wakes up having been turned into a dung-beetle. We are surely not meant to read this as metonymy: it is too unreal. But what does this metaphor signify? A loss of personality? A hideous disfigurement? A self-esteem so low that normal life, normal modes of communication, are impossible?

 Television advertisements have to deliver their message quickly and memorably.

Many use metonymy – happy families, loving couples, smart cars – but many use metaphor, for example a fast animal to suggest the speed of a car. Pay attention to a selection of commercials and note which use metaphor (and how) and which use metonymy. You may find that some use both. Are these the most successful?

Artaud's work was directed at finding ways of integrating metaphor into the theatre (remember the way Artaud used falling limbs and masonry to represent the collapse of civilization).

Working and rehearsal methods

In 1935, Artaud found backing for his Theatre of Cruelty concept, and set about staging Shelley's revenge drama *The Cenci*. In this production, sound effects were frequently synchronised with abrupt lighting changes, sometimes blinding in their intensity. Other elements included enigmatic symbolism; huge masks; stylised facial expressions; intense, frenzied gestures; balletic patterns of movement. The play received only 17 performances and left Artaud facing financial ruin.

Artaud worked from what we would today call 'scenarios', a number of which survive: they are fairly detailed descriptions of what was to happen on stage, but without the prescriptive precision of a script. In order to perform *The Cenci* – which is a verse drama and is rarely performed – Artaud broke the text down, reducing it to a series of extracts. He then built a performance around these extracts. He was relying, in some ways, on the fact that the shape of the drama – if not the details – would be familiar to theatre-goers. He felt that by using familiar stories (or stories with familiar shapes) he could direct his audience away from concern with plot to concern with more meaningful elements. Such an approach demanded a lot from the audience, who were no longer being seen as customers to be entertained. This is part of the thinking behind the choice of name for the project: the Theatre of Cruelty.

In this production of *The Cenci*, Artaud, as one might now expect, used as many theatrical effects as were available to him. Sound was particularly important, and four loudspeakers were used, one in each corner, to deafen the audience with a huge range of recorded effects: 'Tolling bells, screeching machines, echoing footsteps, an oscillating metronome, thunder and lightning, whispering voices in counterpoint, deafening fanfares, ringing anvils, the electronic notes of an ondes martenot.' These sounds were then synchronised with the lighting, which was relatively sophisticated, with floodlights, spotlights and coloured filters.

 Technological change

Today, computer sound-editing programs and other electronic developments make the creation of such 'soundscapes' eas-

When Freud noted his patients' dreams, he turned to metaphor to interpret their concerns, and, notoriously, found sexual imagery in what his patients had dreamt. But was he right to do so? Were these metaphors open to other, very different, interpretations?

Shelley (1792–1822) was a romantic British poet, rather than playwright. His play attracted Artaud in part because of its extreme subject matter: incest, murder, execution and atheism.

Scenarios

Antonin Artaud, 'Production and metaphysics' in *The Theatre and its Double* (Calder 1993).

The ondes martenot is an electronic instrument capable of creating eerie sounds.

ier – and perhaps therefore less startling and dramatic – but it is worthwhile trying to build one for yourself.

- Consider how rhythm and pace can be created by such a soundtrack, as well as the more confrontational effects
- What would Artaud have made of an all-night dance club?

Influence upon other practitioners

Theatre

After Artaud's death in 1948, following disastrous journeys to Mexico and Ireland amid a loss of sanity, there was a gap of nearly twenty years before his ideas gained any new currency. In 1965, Brook's production of *Marat/Sade* by Peter Weiss was presented by the Royal Shakespeare Company in London, using many of Artaud's ideas. Brook went on, in 1968, to direct Seneca's *Oedipus* in London using techniques from the Theatre of Cruelty.

The poet Ted Hughes worked with Brook in preparing the text for *Oedipus*, paring Seneca's original play (which was itself a later adaptation, rather than a translation, of Sophocles' original Greek tragedy) down to the 'basics'. This was a very Artaudian project, with its choice of text, its paring down, its emphasis on ritual and on the collective work of the company to work together on an emotionally and physically demanding piece. Later, in 1971, Brook and Hughes took this one step further by working on a play in Persepolis (with a polyglot company) where Hughes' text was written in a devised language. The communication of the play – its gesture, its visual and aural metaphors, its ritual – was more important than the communication of the script.

> Both the play and the 'language' were called *Orghast*.

Film

Derek Jarman's experimental films of the 1980s, such as *The Last of England,* use techniques that are recognisably Artaud's. There are few opportunities to see productions of Artaud's work, or even of plays in which he had a declared interest, like Strindberg's *Dream Play*. It can be worthwhile, however, to see how a film director like Jarman – consciously or not – came to use in his films methods familiar from Artaud's work. Jarman emphasises imagery more significantly than text. In *The Last of England*, for example, he uses a bonfire on the shore of the Thames as a ritual location, and his performers develop gestures and ritualised patterns of movement that accentuate a metaphorical and almost spiritual significance. The mood of Jarman's work is often anarchic, challenging a bourgeois audience to be shocked by puzzling and sometimes violent imagery.

In these films, Jarman often uses exaggerated lighting effects – darkness, over-exposure, mono-coloration – and a muddy soundtrack full of inexplicable noises and effects. He juxtaposes imagery quite startlingly, so that we are left with the impression of collage.

Further study

Watch Jarman's film version of Shakespeare's *The Tempest.* In what ways is this an Artaudian reading of the play? What does this approach 'uncover'?

Imagine you have your own theatre company in the tradition of Artaud, Brook and Jarman.

Write its manifesto. Ideally, try to devise a piece to perform, but if you don't have time, try to write the reviews which appeared in the next day's papers instead. One of these reviews should be by a critic entirely out of sympathy with what Artaud was seeking to achieve, but the other will be by a critic fully versed in the writings of *The Theatre and its Double* and later developments.

Answering questions on Artaud

The main question on Artaud will ask you to explain one aspect of his ideas. You are being asked to show knowledge and understanding of Artaud's work. This book is a study guide, pointing you in the right direction: it is not a compendium of source material which will replace everything else! To answer on Artaud you need to understand his ideas, which we've outlined here, but you need to have some further familiarity with his writings (especially *The Theatre and its Double*) and ideally with the scripts and scenarios that have survived (including his adaptation of Shelley's *The Cenci* and his later piece *The Conquest of Mexico*). It is helpful to use your own experience as a performer to support your ideas, but you must ensure that your points of comparison are genuine and productive.

 Sample question

Artaud wrote at length in *The Theatre and its Double* on Balinese dance. Explain how he wanted to integrate costume, gesture and ritual into his own theatre.

 Ideas for planning

In your opening paragraph you could explain how Artaud wanted to explore the potential of a new 'language' for the theatre, in which words and speeches played a subordinate part to other theatrical devices such as sound, visual and lighting effects and ritual. You will then be able to link these aims to the key features of Balinese dance. The question focuses on costume, gesture and ritual, so you must too. You can mention sound, for example, in your opening paragraph, because it helps give a context, but then you must leave it.

Try to explain Artaud's theories through a knowledge of his own work. Ensure that every point you make is supported not just by explanation but also by some reference to Artaud's own ideas and practice which have been documented.

• You should here be able to talk about the ways in which gesture in the Balinese performances and in Artaud's own pieces are used to express emotion but whose meaning is often deep and difficult to decode.

• You should be able to draw parallels between the exotic costumes of the Hindu dances and the exaggerated costumes that Artaud championed.

• Discuss how the combination of sound, stylised movement and visual effects in the Balinese dance-dramas is developed in Artaud's thinking into a whole new 'language for the theatre'.

• You should be able to say something about the religious or spiritual overtones to ritual and to much of Artaud's work, which also deals with the mysterious and the ineffable.

- Throughout your answer, you should show close familiarity with Artaud's writings and work, and a willingness at all times to keep to the agenda of the question.

Craig

Why study Craig?

Edward Gordon Craig (1872–1966) was born into a theatrical family in Hertfordshire. His father was Edward William Godwin, an architect and a respected theatre designer in his own right. His mother was Ellen Terry, a famous actress whose support of Craig's projects made them financially viable. She worked extensively as a leading lady in productions by Henry Irving who became a kind of second father to Craig.

Craig's great contribution to the development of European drama lies in his design skills. He designed plays as a whole: set, costumes, performance style, lighting, music – constructing a production rather like an architect views the whole of a building. Today, we might argue, his influence is most obvious, for example, in the productions of grand opera and ballet at the Royal Opera House or the Coliseum, home to English National Opera and English National Ballet. There – in a successful production – design, music and performance all contribute to a memorable and significant whole. Designs are often wildly imaginative, creating impressive and remarkable images out of the available space, and often linked by a surprising but pertinent visual theme. Craig's own designs often employed tricks of perspective, using angled panels and screens or flights of steps, and appeared carefully composed and structured.

From 1908 to 1929 Craig wrote and produced a journal, *The Mask*, devoted to the theatre and itself a lavishly produced work of art. In it, Craig was able to communicate his ideas to an influential list of subscribers.

Theatrical context

Theatre in Britain underwent a significant and profound revival at the end of the 19th century and in the Edwardian era. Between 1880 and 1900, 14 new theatres opened in London alone. Plays at this time depended for their success, by and large, on the presence of a famous leading actor. Such a leading actor, for all intents and purposes, managed the entire production, often in a way which over-emphasised the importance of their role. There was rarely any attempt to design a play as a whole, nor to cast its players on other grounds than stardom and celebrity.

It was through the work of Harley Granville-Barker – playwright and actor – that the modern idea of a 'director' emerged. Barker, working with a company at the Court Theatre, developed an ensemble approach to the playing of realistic drama, with productions that had a considered overall design and mood. In a way, this was the beginning of the end of the leading actor's power in managing productions.

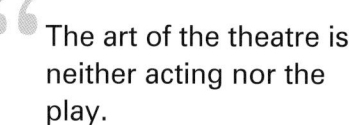

> The art of the theatre is neither acting nor the play.
>
> *The Art of the Theatre*

Further reading

The key text to consider when studying Craig is the section on him in Edward Brown's *The Director and the Stage* (Methuen 1982).

Granville-Barker also published a series of hugely influential 'prefaces' to twelve of Shakespeare's plays.

Developing theatrical purpose

Despite having grown up in an acting family, and despite a number of stage appearances as a child and as a young man, by 1897 Craig had decided to give up acting. He felt he could not achieve the standards set by his mentor, Irving, with whom he had been working in the theatre for eight years. What's more, he had become close friends with two poster artists (James Pryde and William Nicholson, known as the 'Beggarstaff Brothers') and he concentrated his efforts at this time on woodcuts and drawings.

As Craig committed himself to theatre design and production, these artistic skills and talents became more important and significant. He communicated ideas for productions through sketches that captured moments of the play. He designed the visual elements of his dramas with a painter's – or a draughtsman's – eye, and he came, in production, to want to see the play as a series of key moments, each with the potential to be visualised clearly and discretely, like a painting. What's more, his lighting tended to emphasise contrasts and to create the illusions of depth and perspective, just as the shading and hatching of a woodcut or a drawing do.

Theatre and art gallery

Consciously or not, Craig's stage designs reflected the aesthetic values of the painters of his time. Look at the work of current contemporary artists – perhaps this year's Turner Prize shortlist – and consider how you could develop their ideas for use in the theatre.

- What kind of plays would emerge?
- How would a Shakespeare text gain meaning from a production which looked like that?
- What implications are there for the design of the theatre?

Theatre form and stage setting; working methods

Dido and Aeneas

In 1899, Craig persuaded his friend, the musical director Martin Shaw, to stage Purcell's opera *Dido and Aeneas*, rather than to perform it simply as a concert. Craig designed the piece, bearing in mind the limitations of the almost entirely amateur cast. His final designs presented a series of images, used lighting effects imaginatively and were performed on a specially constructed stage. This stage, using canvas and scaffolding, provided a proscenium arch and concealed coloured lighting whose use was particularly effective, especially when projected through hanging gauze. The whole design gave the impression of depth and perspective. This was a radical departure from the usual practice of using a painted backdrop, whereby the realistically painted imagery ironically had the effect of accentuating a production's artificiality.

Art for art's sake

Walter Pater claimed that 'all art constantly aspires towards the condition of music', a phrase used as an epigraph in Craig's book *On the Art of Theatre* in 1905.

Craig's design ideas were of their time. Painters like Whistler, and the 'aesthetic' movement of poet and critic Walter Pater (who preached that art was 'for art's sake') had emphasised the creation of a moody beauty whose meaning was suggested rather than explained. They shared this desire with the French symbolist poets and their aims ran counter to the tradition in Victorian England of

Quoted in 'Edward Gordon Craig', in *The Director and the Stage* by Edward Braun (Methuen 1982).

'genre painting': big set scenes full of narrative and melodrama influenced by the novel.

Craig moved away from the tradition of melodrama and false realism to create a more atmospheric, symbolic setting. As his supporters came to realise, Craig had discovered a new way of approaching classic verse texts. Just as verse is unrealistic but can be dramatically and emotionally effective, so were Craig's designs. As the poet W.B. Yeats observed: 'He created an ideal country where everything was possible, even speaking in verse, or speaking to music, or the expression of the whole of life in a dance.'

Craig's aim was indeed to create on stage a sense of another, idealised world. He spent hours preparing the performance areas where the productions were to take place. For the production of *Dido and Aeneas* he rebuilt the stage area, removing the stepped stage usual for an orchestra and chorus, and replacing it with a one-off long rectangle for performance, viewed through an unusually proportioned proscenium arch. He arranged lighting on a gantry and in the auditorium to replace the conventional footlights. He hung a gauze cloth across the back wall, softening it and avoiding any realistic significance that might be suggested by a backdrop.

In 1901, Craig and Shaw collaborated on another successful Purcell piece, *The Masque of Love*. Craig developed the use of cloth and canvas and of coloured lights. He also used masks which emphasised the stylisation further. Other productions followed. In designing for these shows, Craig was following his own instincts and he was following the experience he had as an artist. But he was also following the important example of the work of Hubert von Herkomer.

Hubert von Herkomer

Web link

Look at Herkomer's painting *Eventide: A Scene in the Westminster Union* (www.liverpoolmuseums.org.uk/ walker/collections/brief_enc/ encounters5.asp). It reveals key features of Craig's distinctive style: the foreground group of characters sit at an angle, subordinated to the overall composition of the piece; the receding, asymmetric lines of perspective create a sense of depth and distance; the window provides back-lighting, turning minor characters into silhouettes.

Herkomer (1849–1914) was an artist who became rich through his portraiture and his illustrations in Victorian novels. He was born in Germany but grew up in Southampton. He developed an interest in designing for the theatre and suggested the use of side lighting to help create mood. It is significant that he wanted to create on stage the atmosphere that contemporary artists were creating in their paintings.

Herkomer's key ideas about stage design focused on creating atmosphere, an atmosphere that would complement the text. He wanted subtler and more varied lighting to replace footlights; he wanted to suggest space and depth through the use of gauzes and coloured cycloramas; he wanted to consider the role of the stage floor itself, its angles and its texture, in building up the mood of the play. Recent advances in technology made possible the use of coloured lighting and even of electric motors to move components of the stage design.

Find out more about Herkomer's paintings and illustrations.

Choose one that seems appropriately atmospheric and that has an appropriately dramatic content. Use your lighting to recreate this scene in your theatre or studio. Think about angles, focus, shadows and colour. Then go on and try to recreate the tableau that Herkomer has painted. You might even want to use this as a starting point for a short piece of original theatre.

These principles of stage design – perspectives and proportion – stayed with Craig throughout his career. In 1906, he worked on a production of Ibsen's *Rosmersholm* in Florence. *Rosmersholm* is one of a series of naturalistic and realistic plays by Ibsen which deals with hypocrisy in society and with the difficulties of sexual relationships. On the page, it does not seem a suitable text for a 'symbolist' style of production. Yet this is what Craig provided, using his hallmark ingredients of cloth hangings, repainting and careful lighting. He added to this costumes that accentuated the mood (at the cost of realism) and a demand of movement which approached that of dance. The result was a triumph. However, when the production moved to a theatre in Nice, the stage manager sawed off the bottom two feet of the set, so it would fit a smaller stage. Craig was apoplectic; he returned to Florence and it was five years before he undertook any more theatrical work.

Rosmersholm

Think about...

How could you redesign your school hall or another traditional performance venue to create a more atmospheric environment? How would Craig, do you think, have approached the same problem?

It is useful to examine how harmonious Craig's vision was with the Symbolist writing of his day. We have already seen how enamoured the poet Yeats was with Craig's work. Here is the opening of Yeats' one-act play *The Player Queen*:

Symbolism

> An open space at the meeting of three streets. One can see for some way down one of these streets, and at some little distance it turns, showing a bare piece of wall lighted by a hanging lamp. Against this lighted wall are silhouetted the heads and shoulders of two Old Men. They are leaning from the upper windows, one on either side of the street. They wear grotesque masks. A little to one side of the stage is a great stone for mounting a horse from. The houses have knockers.

 Sketch out how this scene might appear on stage. Better still, work in a group using whatever is at hand to mock up the set in your own space. Then consider the following questions:

- How does this opening scene setting resemble the style of Craig's work? Think about it as a whole and in detail.
- What is the effect of the use of masks?
- What style of acting would need to be adopted by the cast to make this kind of piece work in a harmonious way?
- You might find it useful to look at Yeats' *Selected Plays* to see the style of writing he adopts. Preparing a rehearsed reading of one of these short plays will help you to understand something about how symbolist theatre works.

See *Selected Plays* by W.B. Yeats, ed. A Norman Jeffares (Papermac 1991).

The director's role

In 1903, Craig worked with his mother (rather miscast at 55 in the starring role of a young Viking wife) on a production of Ibsen's largely ignored play *The Vikings at Helgeland*. It is an unusual play, in that it uses Norse legends and a language halfway between prose and verse to tell a story about jealousy and sexual relationships that was almost shockingly modern. This seems, in hindsight, to be a play rich for Craig's approach. He liked working in the areas between the fantasy of verse and the realism of prose; he created stage designs that looked back to the plain classicism of the ancient theatre but that used modern technology to achieve their effects.

The Vikings at Helgeland

Craig and his company

However, Craig found this work difficult. He did not win the support of the company, neither of the stage management, nor of the actors. His designs were praised – again for their rather other-worldly symbolism and for the moods they created – but the production failed to attract crowds, and was dropped. It was replaced by a production of *Much Ado about Nothing* where, again, Craig's design work did not find harmonious support in the company. Craig appears to have been rather an arrogant man – he was over 30 years old now – and he refused to compromise his plans, even when practical requirements should have obliged him to do so. As it turned out, this was Craig's last venture on the English stage: he spent more or less the rest of his life abroad.

The problem seems to have been a lack of real communication with the cast and the director. While Craig designed a stage set full of atmospheric symbolism, the cast performed in the 'traditional' way, with big stylised speeches delivered to the audience from the prime spots downstage. Craig seems to have been unable to blend his vision of the play as a whole with the performance of the company.

Collaboration with others

This inability to see how the work of the director and of the company must be in harmony with the design in order for the play to succeed was accentuated further in Craig's collaboration with Stanislavski. What should have been one of the greatest collaborations of 20th-century European theatre fell far short of expectations.

Stanislavski

Through Isadora Duncan (see *below*), whom he met in 1904, Craig was invited by Stanislavski to visit Moscow. In autumn 1908 he did so, seeing ten productions by Stanislavski's Moscow Art Theatre. The two men planned a joint production of *Hamlet*. As Stanislavski began rehearsals of the text with his actors, his aim was to present a rather grim realism. He envisaged a military atmosphere, very masculine and oppressive, and based of course on a close reading of a text where guards, soldiers, invasion and fighting are important elements throughout.

In 1909, when the two met for discussions, their work was hindered by two factors. Firstly, they had no language in common except a little German; secondly, they differed fundamentally about the nature of the production. While Stanislavski wanted the kind of realism in the set that would reflect the kind of realism he developed with his company in their acting, Craig saw no need for this, and wanted to reshape the play as a 'monodrama' through Hamlet's eyes, the character appearing on stage throughout. In this disagreement we can see the clash of realism and symbolism.

However, agreement was reached and the production went ahead, with Stanislavski continuing to rehearse realistically and Craig continuing to design symbolically. For this production, Craig focused wholeheartedly on his idea of screens. Although he encountered problems with materials – he could not find (in an age before plastic) any that were both strong enough to stand firm but light enough to be moved – he went ahead to design a production that relied on huge flats being moved to and fro (by stage-hands visible to the audience). Unfortunately, Craig made little or no attempt to embrace the company of actors into his thinking or into his aims for the production and an atmosphere of mutual suspicion prevailed.

Stanislavski, in turn, was becoming exasperated by Craig's attitude (and by his constant demands for payment). In 1912, Craig went to Moscow to attend the final run-throughs and dress rehearsals, but his behaviour during one session was such that he was asked to stay away. In the end, an accident to one of the screens meant they had to be held down by weights, ruining the effect of moving them in view of the audience. Craig's big idea didn't get to happen.

The performance lasted five hours – partly because of the time it took to move the screens with the curtains closed – and was in fact a limited success. However, it was only those scenes where Craig had taken a more 'realistic' approach to design were successful; in this production director and designer did not share the same aims. One member of the Moscow Art Theatre was able to put his finger on Craig's limitations. As a designer he was gifted and creative, 'but when the question concerns directing, then I don't trust him: be he absolutely right, he is too uninterested in acting'. After this project, Craig did little or no work in the theatre; he lived in France until the age of 94.

Quoted in 'Edward Gordon Craig', in *The Director and the Stage* by Edward Braun (Methuen 1982).

The actor: role and training

When Craig first met her, the dancer Isadora Duncan (1878–1927) would perform by improvising dances to contemporary and classical music. Both Craig and Duncan – who was an original and creative performer – believed in the importance of movement to drama. Duncan had achieved both fame and notoriety by rejecting the classical training and demeanour of a ballet-dancer, including the tutu, and dancing barefoot in clothing that clung to her body, revealing rather than concealing its shape and movements.

It is easy to see that a nimble dancer fitted Craig's ideas about stagecraft rather better than a conventional actor. Craig's stage designs required his actors to see themselves first and foremost as props in a carefully-balanced composition. His sketches show the actors as rather secondary elements in the overall design. His enthusiasm for the work of Duncan suggests that he wanted his own actors to be aesthetes, more interested in the beauty of the whole production than in the truth and effectiveness of their own performance. The imprecise meaning of dance seemed to belong much more to the moods Craig created with his set designs than did the precision of an Ibsen text, for example. The deep perspectives and colours that Craig could achieve worked well with dancers, and less well with actors who did not share his vision.

Duncan had found in classical Greek art an ancient inspiration for a modern art. She dressed in the style of the women depicted on Greek vases. She worked on a bare stage (the vases show no background). Her work focused on creating mood and atmosphere rather than, for example, on being politically engaging.

Craig's comments in *The Art of the Theatre* show how he values the constituent parts of a play:

> The art of the theatre is neither acting nor the play, it is not scene nor dance, but it consists of all the elements of which these things are composed: action, which is the very spirit of acting; words, which are the body of the play; line and colour, which are the very heart of the scene; rhythm, which is the very essence of dance.

A marionette is a jointed puppet that is controlled from above by means of strings attached to its limbs. Thus what Craig proposes is literally a 'super-puppet'. He is using a German word knowing that readers will pick up the reference to Nietshe's idea of a heroic man or 'Übermensch' (superman).

In his preface to a new edition of *The Art of the Theatre*, published in 1924, Craig seems to argue that actors should be replaced by a kind of intelligent automaton, which he called the 'Über-Marionette'. Whatever he meant by this precisely – and many critics have analysed the idea backwards and forwards over the years – the general drift is obvious. Craig saw a play as a series of atmospheric, memorable and painterly scenes, linked by fluent and essentially sensual movement. In such an environment, acting skills – the skills of developing a character and of creating a role – are far from significant. One can imagine Craig replacing a text with music, so that the whole issue of delivering a text is gone. Inevitably, for such a project, Craig wants a talented individual who is not concerned with developing his or her own ideas about acting: in other words, the Über-Marionette.

Answering questions on Craig

The main question on Craig will require you to know facts about Craig's career and productions. To answer well on Craig you need to understand his ideas, which we've outlined here, and you need to have some further familiarity with his designs. It may be helpful to use your own experience as a designer to support your ideas, but you must ensure that your points of comparison are genuine and productive.

Date	Production	'Signature features' present	Other comments
1900	*Dido and Aeneas* (London)	Production conceived as a series of composed symbolist-style images, often employing striking colour contrasts, coloured lighting and the effects of chiaroscuro (light and dark effects). Creation of a 'false' proscenium arch with scaffolding and canvas. Radical approach to lighting using a gantry concealed behind this false arch, as well as other lights concealed in the set and in the auditorium. No overhead lamps or footlights. At the rear of the stage a gauze was hung in front of a grey and a blue cloth, creating, when lit with coloured light, the sense of great depth.	This was the production which set out the principles on which Craig's career hung and developed.
1901	*The Masque of Love* (London)	Symbolist predominance of style over detail developed further. A light grey canvas background and coloured coarse costumes were used to construct impressive visual compositions. Performers' movements were rhythmic and unrealistic. Use of carefully plotted coloured lighting.	The sketchy plot of this production meant that the design could take precedence: Craig found it difficult later to reconcile his design ideas with more powerful plays and with stronger performers.
1902	*Acis and Galatea* (London)	No attempt to suggest the 'real' setting. Lengths of cloths used to create shadows and mood. Shadows projected on to a deep blue backcloth as the lovers were lit with deep red light. A final cascade effect was created using a cloth pierced with holes and moving perforated discs behind, through which the lights shone.	The cascade trick was adapted from a pantomime device employed at the Princess's Theatre.